Ahab & **Jezebel**

JAMIE CLAGUE

CREATION
HOUSE

Ahab and Jezebel: A Bunch of Guaranteed Ways to
Ruin Your Marriage by Jamie Clague
Published by Creation House
A Charisma Media Company
600 Rinehart Road
Lake Mary, Florida 32746
www.charismamedia.com

Unless otherwise noted, all Scripture quotations are from
New International Version. Copyright © 1973, 1978, 1984,
2010, 2011, International Bible Society. Used by permission.

Unless otherwise noted, the persons used as examples in
this book are fictitious. Any resemblance to actual people,
whether living or dead, is coincidental.

Design Director: Justin Evans
Cover design by Judith McKittrick Wright.
Illustrations by Austin Schuster

Visit the author's website: jamieclagueministries.com.

Library of Congress CataloginginPublication Data:
2014956291
International Standard Book Number: 978-1-62998-412-4
E-book International Standard Book Number:
978-1-62998-413-1

First edition

15 16 17 18 19 — 987654321
Printed in Canada

This book is dedicated to my rock, my husband, Jim, who has walked out this testimony with me.

To my precious daughters, Halie, Brityn, and Lindsy; thank you for your forgiveness where I have failed you and for your encouragement on this journey. I adore you.

To my momma who hung in there in the hardest of circumstances and, like me, wishes better for the marriages of our children and their children.

To all of the long-suffering people who have poured into my marriage and given Jim and me great mentoring.

And to my darling friend Chris, for loving me enough to tell me to stop!

To my Savior, Jesus Christ, for going before me and making a way. I love You, O my King!

CONTENTS

INTRODUCTION

*M*Y PRECIOUS SISTER in Christ, if you have this book in hand, know that I am with you. Know that He is with you. If your marriage is in shambles or if you are just really ready for growth in your relationship, this book is for you. I am *not* a counselor. I am a woman who has walked a very long, difficult path in my own marriage. I do not want the same for you. I want you to know there is hope and there is a different way.

I started this book with the intent of sharing a deep study on the "Jezebel spirit." My Savior tricked me! He had another plan. This has ended up being like, for lack of better words, a Bernstein Bears book: you know, where the dad keeps saying, "Son, let me show you how this is done." And then he commences to make a total mess of the whole thing. Well, that is me. That is this very book.

Most of the stories are mine; some of them are from other people. I have changed the names and circumstances to protect their privacy.

I am going to be honest with you, brutally honest. I might push you past your ability to believe. I might dig so deep that you need healing. I might take you *way* out of your comfort zone. I might make you laugh your head off. I might make you cry. I know I will make you mad! I might share some stuff that is so awful that you feel great about the condition of your marriage. I only know God put this on my heart...for me...for you.

He knows. He knows I needed *my* husband for *my* growth. I *did not* like that. I *do not* like that. If you are willing to go to a hard place with me, *He* will show you how to grow—not only as a wife but also as a woman with a heart for Him.

Let's go girl!

Chapter 1

BROKEN COVENANT

Ahab and Jezebel

I DECIDED

*J*UNE 2004 IS when I did "it"; *I decided.* I remember the minute it happened. My precious daddy had committed suicide three weeks prior. My emotions had never been rawer. When you have lost someone precious in your life, it makes the relationships that remain more crucial to you. In my case I became desperate for deeper, richer relationships with all whom I love.

Our marriage had always been a rocky one. We were pregnant and married at seventeen and eighteen years old. By the time I was twenty-three we had three children. I came to know Christ after about ten years of marriage. Having a teen marriage and being unequally yoked were only a couple of the issues. We struggled financially, had a lack of communication skills, had differences in parenting, etc., etc., etc. Over the years, we had been to several Christian counselors, pastors, Bible studies, and mentors for help in our marriage.

So, three weeks after burying a tiny box with my daddy's ashes in it, *I decided*. *I decided* that my marriage of twenty-seven years was going to change. You see, I had spent the last twelve years ministering, for the most part, to my husband in a godly way. I was submissive, loving, kind, and forgiving; but "it" wasn't "working." He still didn't love the Lord and was still angry and controlling. I must tell you that I was obeying the Lord with a motive. My motive was for my own comfort in my marriage, for my personal gain of a better life, and to change my husband—icky.

It was "time" to fix everything crooked in my marriage…because *I decided*. *I decided* that *I* would not allow another loved one in my life to go to the grave without rich full relationship with *me*…especially my husband. *I decided* we were going to love one another. *I decided* we were going to cherish each moment together because we are not promised the next moment. *I decided* we would treat each other with love and respect. *I decided* we would seek God together. *I decided* we would love on our kids like never before and let them know how deeply they are loved. *I decided* the time had come and we were going to fix this marriage—now! *I decided*, whether my husband liked it or not! My motives were pure, my heart right, and my goals godly. Ladies, this is the day; the day *I went my own way*.

Can I tell you what that looked like to the Lord?

> They have chosen their own ways, and their souls delight in their abominations; so I also will choose harsh treatment for them and will bring upon them what they dread. For when I called, no one listened. They did evil in my sight and chose what displeases me.
>
> —ISAIAH 66:3–4

You see, ladies, God has a plan for my marriage and for your marriage. When we go around telling Him what to do and how it is going to go, we are in sin. I stayed in that sin for almost seven years. I stopped loving on my husband, I started correcting everything he did, I stopped ministering to him, I started preaching to him, I did not let one thing go, I confronted *everything*; because I *decided*.

Do you think you were born with a marriage manual in your head? Do you have expectations in your heart for your marriage that you have kept secret yet you punish your husband for not fulfilling them? Have you broken marriage covenant with selfishness, hate, bitterness, contentiousness, shutdown, or a certain behavior you justify?

Seven years later I had a dead marriage. Before it was problematic, now it was dead in the water. I had managed to destroy any good thing we had had previously. I had ruined my godly example to my unbelieving husband. Way to go, Jamie!

I Fell

But God! Oh, isn't He *always* restorative and redemptive? After seven years with a dead marriage and a walk with Christ that was in shambles, I fell. I fell to my knees and begged my King to show me. Where had I gone wrong? Why was my marriage dead? Why, why, why? And there was Isaiah: you have gone your own way. Yes I had. I broke before Him in repentance. Then my sweet Savior took me to Psalm 32.

If you want deep change in yourself and in your marriage, this is part of that change. If you are sensing in your spirit already that you have gone your "own way" in your marriage, will you put this book down and ask Christ to show you what you have done (or not done) that is "going your own way" in your marriage? Then repent. Then, with a highlighter go to Psalm 32, read it with Him, receive His forgiveness, and go on. I am going to do this several times during this book, and I beg of you to follow through.

The precious Lord began speaking to my heart through this psalm: "Jamie, you are forgiven. I do not count this against you. You were afflicted with pain when you went your own way. But you came to Me and confessed; and I, the Lord, will forgive you.

I will hide you and help you if you will go with Me, not ahead of Me. My unfailing love is yours."

I got what I desired: unfailing love; my Savior's unfailing love, no matter where I had been—for a very, very long time.

So what does God want of you in your marriage? Let's see.

Jeremiah 11:3–8 uses these words to describe covenant. Our God is a God of covenant, and He takes it very seriously: "Cursed is the one who does *not* obey the terms of this covenant" (v. 3, emphasis added). Did you stand before the Lord and a multitude of other people on your wedding day and *vow* to love, honor, cherish, and maybe even *obey* your precious husband? Yes or no? Verse 4 tells us: "I said, obey me and do *everything* I command you" (emphasis added). Are you doing everything the Word and the Spirit asks you to do or not do in your marriage?

The Lord goes on to say what He will do: "I *will…give* [you] a land flowing with milk and honey" (v. 5, emphasis added). So, He tells us there are good things *if* we will not break covenant. "Listen to the terms of this covenant and follow them" (v. 6); are we listening to the Holy Spirit about our marriages? Are we following? In verse 7 the Lord tells us: "I warned them again and again." How many times has the King warned you? He warned me plenty, but I would not listen. Continuing in verse 7 the Lord says, "Obey me."

Verse 8 explains the response: "But they did not listen or pay attention; *instead, they followed the stubbornness of their evil hearts*" (emphasis added). Ouch! They *went their own way*. Not only ouch, but yikes! Have you ever read the Old Testament and proudly thought, "Oh, I would *never* do that!" Obey Christ, listen, pay attention, and do *not* follow your stubborn heart. I did. I paid deeply for it. I am still paying for some of it as the Lord does the redeeming, healing work in my marriage. We break covenant (marriage covenant) through anger, resentment, rebellion, infidelity, secrecy, bitterness, control, and a myriad of other ungodly ways. We do. We *all* do. We go our own way.

ENTERTAINING GUESTS

So many times in broken covenant marriages I see two people. These two people do not have skin on; they are spiritual. They like to inhabit married couples and wreak havoc on their relationship. These people are gender distinct (female/male) with skin on (human), and in the Bible. However, we see their "persons" or "personalities" show up in both males and females. For sake of this book, we will entertain these two in their familiar genders. Who are you entertaining? Let's take a look at who's coming to dinner.

Knock, knock. Who's there? It's Jezzy. Jezzy who? Jezzy "let me mess up your marriage a bit"; that's who. Oh! Come on in.

Let's take a look at who you are entertaining this evening. I say "entertain" because she has not "attacked" you the way a demon might. *You* have opened the door, invited her in, sat her down, and entertained her.

Before you go onto the next chapter, I would love for you to dig into the latter portion of 1 Kings and the first several chapters of 2 Kings to get to know Jezebel better. She is referred to again in the Book of Revelation. Use your concordance and really get to know her ways and her heart. Then check to see if you have entertained her in any way. Watch her ways of manipulation; hear her words and her attitudes toward her husband. Now remember, you may not have invited Jezzy to dinner; it may be your husband that has entertained her. But, more often than not, this little lady is *us*.

The first time I knew I was entertaining a "Jezebel spirit" I was at a Bible study. It was early on in my walk with the Lord. I was arguing with several points in the study when a young lady turned to me and stated, "Jamie, you are *so* unteachable!" I felt the words go through my chest (the two-edged sword) and out my back. To this day, when I feel that, I know it is the Lord "slaying" my spirit with a hard truth that needs to get through me.

Jezzy is unteachable; she does not listen; she talks *way* too much or *way* too little; and she is sharp- or smooth-tongued, manipulative, controlling, defensive, seductive, critical, and very needy. She needs to be seen, heard, and obeyed. Her root sin is rebellion against the King, which manifests itself in many ways; but mostly it manifests as rebellion or pride against the Most High God.

You say, "But Jamie, I do not do any of these things. I would never..." Really? Do you use a sarcastic tone when you address your husband's mistakes? Do you make all of the decisions? Do you make him make all of the decisions? Do you tell him when he is wrong—all of the time? Are you hyper spiritual and sweet, and do you always do the "right" thing so your husband can see you and learn? Do you withhold sex? Do you discourage him and not encourage him? Maybe you just hate men in general because of past abuse or issues. Do you threaten or think of divorce often? Do you use the silent treatment, shutdown, or pouting to manipulate? Ask the Lord, sister; ask Him to show you if you are entertaining Jezzy anywhere in your marriage. If you are having difficulty in your marriage right now, I can tell you someone is entertaining her. God does not take Jezzy lightly.

Tummy tuck

I suffered from a Jezzy decision in a mighty way many years ago. You see, we can walk free from her for long periods of time and then, bam! there she is. For many years I desired to have a tummy tuck. Yes, I had plastic surgery; no shame, just pain. And, besides, God made plastic surgeons. I was left a small inheritance from a relative. I decided I would minister to myself with the long-awaited tuck.

I brought the idea before my husband, and he said he would think about it. I'm thinking, "What do you have to think about? I have the money." He came back to me and asked if I would wait another year—until the next spring because of extenuating circumstances. I did not seek the Lord. Jezzy does not seek the Lord; she goes her own way. I thought about it for a few days and went back to my husband with the issue. He again asked if I would wait. I matter-of-factly said, "No, I have waited *so* long and I really want it now since I have the money." He acquiesced. Jezzy does not listen to her husband.

I had the surgery with my husband at my side. The anesthesia went wrong, and I seized for two hours before waking up. I nearly bled to death from a "bleeder." I had to have the surgery done all over the next day. My recovery was twelve weeks, not four to six. In that time I suffered from fluid under my skin that had to be extracted via four-inch needles. I wore drainage tubes for three weeks instead of one. I had the drainage tubes adhere to my insides so they had to be ripped out forcibly. And, I had many other horrific consequences.

On about week number eight, as I lay/sat (the skin is pulled so tight you cannot lay flat) in bed (awake as the pain pills wore off), I wept and cried out to the Lord, "Why Lord? Why am I still in horrific pain and have had all of these complications?"

His reply was loud, clear and sharp: "I gave you your king." And He repeated, "I gave you your king." Oh, my sisters, just like when the people of the Old Testament insisted God give them a king rejecting Him as their leader (1 Sam. 8:6-7), I too insisted on that tummy tuck—*my way*.

Revelation 2:22 says, "I will cast her on a bed of suffering." Precious one, I was on one of the worst beds of physical suffering I had ever experienced. I had made a Jezzy decision. I did *not* honor my husband. I broke covenant. Are you able to see more clearly now any areas you may be operating arm in arm with Ms. Jezzy?

Along comes Ahab

Remember, we are talking about couples here. When you opened that door for your dinner guests, there was Jezz. And then behind her you will find Ahab. I would bet no one has ever met a couple that has a Jezzy without an Ahab. See, Jezzy does not do well unless she has an Ahab. This gal goes out and seeks out her Ahab. Now, I do not want to infer that Jezzy "people" do this consciously. In fact, you might even be denying it right now. Many times the Jezzy "in us" is looking and pointing out these Ahabs and we are not even aware of it. Honestly, for Jezzy to be effective, she really *needs* an Ahab. Keep in mind that there are reversals; I have seen Jezzy men with Ahab women.

You will also find the stories of Ahab along with Jezebel mostly in 1 and 2 Kings. Let me give you just a little peek at Ahab. He willingly married a woman who worshipped Baal; he *knew* what he was getting into. Ahab is a man of weak standards; he compromises, a lot. Ahab's "god" is comfort; he doesn't want to deal with confrontation. His wife was out killing the prophets of God and he was at home worrying where he was going to put the cattle she "pilfered" and how to feed them (1 Kings 18:4–5). It was a strain on their own livestock—ho hum, oh well. He continues on to blame Elijah instead of his wife (v. 16), and then he goes off to eat and drink. Ahab ministers to himself and the lust of ease.

Men caught in Ahab will avoid confrontation—at any cost. Ahab then gets really bummed out and goes to bed—for a long time. He goes into shutdown, pulls the covers over his head, and hides (21:4). Oh, but Ms. Jezzy finds him, rebukes him instead of encouraging him, and then *she* goes and does *his* job (vv. 5–16). She *proves* to him what a weak man he is. Nice.

When Jezzy does stuff that is her husband's responsibility, she usurps his authority. (Remember my husband's position on my tummy tuck? *He* acquiesced; *he* gave in). She "fixes" everything for her little man; and then, God. God holds Ahab accountable for not leading his wife, home, and people. Ahab has given his authority to his wife by not leading. She *cannot* take it from him without him *allowing* it. Men who will not lead in their home have opened the door to Ahab, ushered him in, and seated him at the rear of their dinner table. He allows Jezzy to be at the head.

This man will not lead spiritually. He will hand over most decisions to his wife. He will have many outside interests or be detached so he doesn't have to be involved. Or he may be super dependent on his wife and her opinions.

Ice fishing

I watched a group of young men ice fishing today. If you do not understand this phenomenon, I will explain. In this north country of Minnesota, it can get to 30 degrees below or more. This means our lakes freeze solid, maybe up to two or three feet thick. It is thick! Then people go out on the lake driving a truck or car or maybe walking. They cut a hole and maybe put a little house over it and fish. So these young men pulled all of their gear, on foot, out onto the ice. They set up the tent thingamajig, the rod and reel thingamajig, and the cutting table. They then cut holes in the ice, opened buckets, started up warming thingamajigs, etc. After all of this they proceeded to fish.

About a half hour later, I saw the strangest thing. They started to run to pack it all up and move the whole deal about 100 feet away. They set up the tent thingamajig, the rod and reel thingamajig, and the whole kit and caboodle all over again. Get the picture? Then about an hour later they did the same thing again. I was amazed! They worked in unison and *ran* to get the job done.

So, like I do, I started to talk to the Lord about that. I said, "Lord, there is so much enthusiasm, preparation, and passion in these young men. Their wives are desperate for that in their marriages. What's the deal, Lord?" As the Holy Spirit and I continued to watch this production, He answered me, "It is because it fulfills them and they *feel* successful." Wow!

Do you have an Ahab in your life who needs to be fulfilled and feel successful? Do you want your man to run with preparedness, enthusiasm, and passion for you and your marriage? He will *if* Jezzy will stop. Stop, stop, stop whatever it is you may be doing or not doing to control your relationship. Stop! Jezebel has a fear of losing control. Ladies, God created us to be a "helper"; we've manufactured a "manipulator." If you see yourself anywhere in this book, check the Word, ask your Savior, ask your husband, and ask your friends to be honest with you about the areas you may be entertaining her. Ahab must start to lead. Ahab has a fear of failure. However, he *will* start to lead when you *stop*. It is a "God" thing, *if* we let it happen.

Chapter 2

CAN'T OR WON'T?

Acknowledge the God of your father, and serve
him with wholehearted devotion and with a
willing mind, for the Lord searches every heart
and understands every motive behind the thoughts.

1 CHRONICLES 28:9, EMPHASIS ADDED

ONLY THE LORD knows the hearts and motives of men—meaning mankind, us. This chapter is going to bruise your pride a bit, especially if you have sidled up to Ms. Jezzy. Remember, she "thinks" she knows all things. Can we take a look at the truth? Oh good; God likes that—the truth. You see, we have this crazy dialogue with ourselves about our husbands: "He *knows* I don't like that. I *know* he heard me; he just doesn't listen. If it were important to *him*, he would do it right away. He just doesn't care about *my* needs." On and on we go...again.

In this chapter I am going to help you explore what you *don't* know and how to deal with what you *do* know. The first thing you need to ask yourself before the Lord is, "Lord, will You show me what I really don't know?" If you do not want to go there, then go get in your prayer closet and ask Jesus to help you to confront your pride and control issues. Unwillingness to look at ourselves is one of the first red flags of pride.

LOVE

So, as I am growing in the Lord, I come to the realization that I only "think" I know what love is. My list was fairly short but very relational and spiritual. I decided that if the Word was true and our instruction manual, then God would for sure include His description of love. I went to my concordance to see what God said about love, and there it was—*love!* I looked up all of the scriptures on love. My question was, "Lord, will You give me Your description of love?" What is love? Ladies, I don't know what your theology is, but I do know this: you can ask your Creator anything—anything.

Before you go on, go get a piece of paper and write down in all honesty what love between you and your husband would look like to you if it were "perfect." You done? Now set that aside. If you are not stopping during the reading of this book, especially where I have suggested it, it may mean a few things: (1) you are so excited to have all of the answers to fix your marriage that you aren't being patient enough to stop, (2) you really don't want to do the hard work of restoring your marriage to God's design, or (3) you haven't received that these "time outs" are not me bossing but the Holy Spirit prompting. Check it out. Ask the Lord if He wants you to "dig in" at these places. Maybe you have a different reason that is legitimate. I don't know. If so, bless you.

I was totally open to receive the fact that I may truly not even know what love was. And I didn't! Because I am very black and white in my thinking, I was drawn to the very clear scripture that says, "Love is..." Yep, 1 Corinthians 13:4–7 says,

> Love is patient, love is kind [am I?]. It does not envy, it does not boast, it is not proud [am I not?]. It is not rude, it is not self- seeking, it is not easily angered, it keeps no record of wrongs [do I, or do I not?]. Love does not delight in evil but rejoices with the truth. It always protects, always trusts, always hopes, always perseveres.
>
> *O God! I don't even know, according to Your Word, what love is and is not. I know nothing. Teach me, O Lord.*

I so desired to know love from Christ's perspective that I dug into this scripture. I looked at every word, looked at the cross-references, and took equal note of the "does" and "is's" and "nots." I sought the truth.

My point here, sweet sisters, is that many times when you or your spouse seems to be unwilling to "do" something or "be" a certain way, it is *not* because we *won't*, it may be because we *can't*. It wasn't that I *wouldn't* love my husband; I *couldn't*. I did not have the true understanding or the tools to know how. Remember, I was digging from a well of dysfunction from my own past.

Many of us do not have a healthy well to draw from. Think of the great pride we are in when we conjure up the "marriage should be, he should be, we should be's," when we are inept ourselves. I cannot say this enough: get healthy, godly women in your life and beg them to pray over you.

After studying the scripture on love, praying, and "trying" to "love" on my husband, I realized that I was just walking it but not really embracing it and allowing it to change me. After doing all I knew to do, I reached out. I went to Janet. After my best friend, Terry (I owe her my life; she brought me to Him), it was Janet who discipled me. She grew me up. She taught me principles in my walk that I walk by today—balanced, God-seeking principles.

We went into prayer for my marriage and my lack of "heart" change in the area of love. Janet always "listened" to the Holy Spirit. She would seek Him and then wait. I loved that then, and I walk in it now. When we ask God a question, it is a good idea to wait for His answer. After a few minutes she asks me to sit in a chair she has pulled into the middle of the kitchen (this is also a great idea). The Word says we are to stand in the gap (Ezek. 22:30) for one another, and she did. With her hand on my back, the Holy Spirit began to speak to her: "Jamie, the Lord is showing me a root; it goes in the top of your head all the way down to your midsection. It is like a root, a deep root. You have a deep root of bitterness toward your husband and God."

Bitterness is rooted in unforgiveness, ladies; and unforgiveness is sin. I repented. As the root was removed from me, I felt the Lord filling the deep hole with grace, mercy, and forgiveness. When I had a "can't," my Jesus gave me grace, mercy, and forgiveness. I went home that evening and sat my unbelieving, angry husband down and told him, "I am sorry for rejecting and not loving you. It isn't because you are a bad man. It is because I didn't know how to love you. Please forgive me."

So, the "can'ts" are where we all are in one area or another. Let me repeat that: the *"can'ts"* are where we *all* are in one area or another. Will you see the grace and mercy in that? Will you look at the areas in your life that you have to stand before the Lord and say, "Daddy, I know You want me to do this (or stop this), but I don't know how. I can't without You." This precious Savior of ours will meet us there.

Like a tender daddy, He will reach down and pull you to His lap and show you the way to go.

In the same light, will we, when our husbands have an area of "can't," extend grace and mercy? Really? Did you just race off on the old "he *knows...*" race track? Only God knows the hearts and motives of men, Ms. J.

For those of you who have shed your robe of pride and feel naked before the Lord right now, don't worry. He will clothe you with His humility so that you are able to distinguish the can'ts or won'ts in your life and your spouse's life. Be so humble and so seeking that you will allow the Holy Spirit to show you.

I was going to share with you the times the Lord showed me that my husband was a "can't," but my journal is full of them. You see, without Jesus he really can't.

CAN'TS AND FORGIVENESS

Several years ago, the Lord showed me one of my husband's "can'ts" in the most touching way. We were attending a marriage conference. Yes, I dragged him to it. The "assignment" that afternoon was to get alone with your spouse and write them a letter about how you were feeling as you walked down the aisle on your wedding day. The point was to remember all of the precious reasons you chose this person as your life mate. (I suggest you do this.)

We sat in our car as the wind was blowing like mad outside. He started to write in his workbook. I sat and stared at mine. I was afraid to "go there." I prayed silently, "Father, take me back there. What Lord? What?" I saw myself, a seventeen-year-old pregnant girl, walking down the aisle, meeting him in front of the candelabra. I distinctly remember looking at him and thinking, "He, unlike my dad, will be *nice* to me."

The memory brought up the reality that our marriage had been very different than what that young girl hoped for. The pain was so intense I thought I would go into the give-me-a-towel cry. I bawled and bawled. I could not put pencil to paper. I just openmouth bawled.

My husband looked at me, worried that I was having a "for real" breakdown right there in the parking lot. "Are you OK?" he ventured. After several minutes, I hurled, "I can't write this! I saw you as my safe place and that you would be nice to me. And you are *not*!" I am bawling into a tissue because I didn't bring my bawl towel. He is sitting in silence, tears streaming down his face.

The grieving subsiding, I heard my Abba's voice, "Jamie, Jim was not maliciously mean to you and the girls; he knew *no other way*." There was a long pause: "Will you forgive him?" I looked and listened to what my Abba was telling me and showing me. You see, the well that my husband had drawn from in his past was vile and distant. He knew nothing else; he knew not his King.

Again the Lord asked, "Will you forgive him?" "No, I can't!" I yelled back in my head. "I will help you," the Lord prodded. "I can't, I can't, I can't! Oh please, God, don't ask me to do this." I wrestled. I had "forgiven" my husband the daily hurts, but *this* forgiveness, this deep all-encompassing forgiveness, felt too big for me.

Then the truth flooded my heart. My Jesus would never ask me to do something that would harm me. "I will forgive him out of obedience to You, Lord; but I don't *feel* forgiving," I responded in my head. I lifted my eyes to my husband, still crying in the seat next to me. "Jim, I forgive you," I say flatly. He just stares at me. The Holy Spirit says, "Again, Jamie." "Jim, I forgive you," I say more genuinely.

Ah, there it is; the washing of the Holy Spirit. I am now flooded with Him, His heart, His forgiveness. "One more time, Jamie." "Jim, I *forgive* you for being mean to me and the girls. I forgive you, I forgive you, I forgive you!" With every word of forgiveness, my being was cleansed, lifted, and brought up, up, and up. (Sweet daughter of the Most High, often God's blessing comes *after* your obedience.) I am now sporting a broad smile of freedom. He is staring, incredulous. "How do you *do* that?" he exclaims.

You see, precious sisters, it is not "how" I could do that? It was "why." Why would I do such a thing?

Because I *could* because of Him. Sometimes the "won'ts" and "can'ts" get very clouded. If we are seeking God, He will help us to muddle through.

So, the "can'ts" are full of mercy and grace. A "can't" is more of an inability or lack of tools. A "can't" has taken root in the center of who we are, and we don't even know why.

HONORING NO

How about the "won'ts"? Well, yeah, that is a whole different story. A "won't" is a choice. The grace and mercy of God in these "won't" events is also evident. He is so just that He allows us choice. This is a God that honors our "no." Doesn't that just blow your mind?

About ten years into our marriage I read a "marriage helper" book that taught the principles of using "word pictures" to communicate with your spouse. Soon after I had finished the book, I had a situation that came up in my marriage that needed to be addressed. I knew a word picture would be perfect for my very visual man. Being so not visual but very literal, this picture thing was *way* out of my comfort zone and ability. I asked the Lord to give me a word picture to share my concern with my husband. He, as always, was faithful.

The picture He gave me was of a fork in the road. At the intersection you could go left or right, but not forward. I saw myself at the intersection in our awesome wood-grain paneled station wagon. (Don't complain about your van.) In my vehicle were myself, my kids, food, crafts, baseballs, Bibles, beach gear, and the dog. As I approached the "juncture," I put on my blinker, *sure* of which way to go. My husband is *following* (Ms. J's got this) in his truck. The contents of his vehicle include our savings, TV, checkbook, fishing tackle, recliner, and a lawn mower. He slowly pulls up close behind me. As I observe in the rearview mirror, amazingly he goes in the other lane and puts on his blinker for the *opposite* direction. Needless to say, I am devastated at his *choice* of going the opposite way of our family, having the lawn mower and TV as his greatest importance and money as his guide.

How's that for a girl that is not creative or visual? God is good! So I share my "picture" with my husband that evening. He is very appreciative for the word picture, and states that it helped him very much to understand and "see" my position without feeling chastised. Whew! For several weeks he is extra attentive to our children and me and seems to be more attached than his usual detached self— for several weeks.

Fast-forward: today he is detached, yet less detached; a work in God's hands. The consequences for his choices have been shallow relationships with his children, loss of intimacy in his marriage, and lack of relationship with his Savior. I am so sorry if that removes all hope for you. But God! God has given *me* a rich relationship with my children, Him, and others. You see, my motive for what I do cannot be to *change* him. My motive has to be obedience unto the Lord. My husband chose a different road that day. So what do I do with that? I *honor* it. Sweet darlin', I honor his "no." I will tell you why.

Remember Janet? Well, one day she had a "word" for my husband. She said to him, "Jim, the Lord told me to tell you that He will go as fast or slow as you want." The King of the universe will allow my husband to choose the pace. Years later I had a vision of my husband walking along a dusty road on a very hot day. He was carrying a very heavy yoke across his shoulders. I was just about to pray for the Lord to lift the yoke that was burdening my husband when I took a "broader" look at the vision. Walking alongside my husband was our sweet Savior, tears running down His face as my husband carried the load alone and would not hand it over. Our King, our Savior, was honoring my husband's "no." Who am I, sister, to not honor another's no?

The road to understanding this phenomenon has been a long, arduous one for me. It took many, many years for me to finally "hear" the no's and to honor them. Please do not misunderstand the term "honoring his no." I would *never* ask a woman to honor a "no" in any kind of abusive relationship. If you are in one, seek help. If you have gone around and around the same issue and it does not change, I am sorry, sister, his answer is no. He has decided. You need to "honor" his clear decision of no and seek godly counsel on where your next turn will be.

Help from professionals

I reached out to a Christian radio program one day for such help. This program is heard worldwide with professional Christian men and women available for counsel. I called in; and to my amazement, got on the show. I was put on hold for a while, so as I waited I was asking the Lord to speak through these people about how I could deal with the loneliness in my marriage. For twenty-five years I had brought my desires to the table for communication, seeking God together, and shutting off the TV. We had just made a cross-country move, and I was lonelier than I had ever been. The line clicked in. "Hi, this is Peter Professional on *We Can Help*. How can we help you today?" he chimed. My heart was racing, not because I was nervous but I was so excited to have these way godly men with so much experience speaking into my difficulty. I *knew* I was going to get a fix for the loneliness in my marriage. Finally!

I spoke my desire clearly, "Well, I have been married for twenty-five years and I have been asking my husband to talk to me, pray with me, and shut the TV off. Now we have moved where I know no one and it is worse than ever. What can I do? I keep asking and asking." Without a pause, both of the "pros" yell, "Stop asking!" I thought I heard them wrong; "Pardon?" And again they *both* say, "Stop asking. Jamie, his answer is *no*." I felt the blood drain out of my face and a pit begin to form in my belly. The radio personnel rambled on about getting my own activities and life. They are oblivious that I have gone into full despair. The conversation ends with, "We are so glad to have been able to help you today, Jamie. Thank you for calling *We Can Help*."

I dropped to my knees in hopelessness. I allowed the enemy to take me down the "it's over" trip. After all, if we weren't going to do stuff together, pray together, and have deep intimate conversations together, then there is no marriage. Right? I wept it out and surrendered *my* expectations and dreams I had about how our marriage was going to be. Now released, I was able to absorb what they told me I needed to do. They were right. How dumb could I be? When you ask someone to do something for twenty five years and they don't; hello, it's a no! If you ask someone to stop something repeatedly and they don't, it is a no. Why was I not listening to his no?

As the truth sunk in, I scraped myself up off of the floor. I wrestled for days with what my new life would look like. I began to understand that happiness in my life was not on my husband but on me and me alone. I embraced my new plan to "get a life." Is it sad that I have to pursue relationships to fill my cup? Yes, sad. Devastating? No. Remember, when people make "won't" decisions there is always a consequence. Consequences help us grow. My husband sits home alone often because I heard his no and let him stay detached.

No thanks

I had a great lesson in honoring someone's "no" the other day. I was in Larry's Lumber buying some paint. Keep in mind I used to own my own wallpaper/painting business. I was in the process of selling my home and was ridding the spare bedroom of my husband's favorite (hideous) hunter green/maroon décor. In the paint aisle I sought out the least expensive gallon of paint they had. The clerk approached me and inquired, "Do you need some assistance?" "No thanks," I replied, continuing to compare. I grabbed the $11.99 per gallon and walked toward the brushes. Mr. Clerk sees the paint and says, "Oh Ma'am, you don't want to use that paint; it is the cheapest we have." "I'm OK with it; thanks, though," I respond.

"You need a brush?" he asks. Duh, that is why I am standing in front of them, Mr. I-don't-need-help! "Yep," I curtly answer and turn my body away from him. (In case you don't know, this means "go away," in body language.) I choose, again, an inexpensive brush. "Oh, Ma'am, you don't want that brush; it is the cheapest we have. I don't think you are going to be happy with it," he directs.

I get to the counter and he asks what I am painting. I tell him. Then he says, "You really should have a tarp, some tape, and an edger." I very evenly say, "Sir, I am painting a room in a home I am about to sell; so I really don't care if I purchase high quality anything." My eyes locked on his. He backs down, "Oh, sorry; I didn't mean to push."

I am normally very patient. Not so much that day. I got in my car and realized that even though I had not been outright rude, I was *really* rude in my heart. (Note: when you have elevated emotions—anger, fear, sadness, etc.—ask yourself why. God uses emotions to show us what we need to "look" at.) "Lord, why did that bother me so much?" I kind of whined. Clearly He responded, "Because he wouldn't honor your 'no'." Can I tell you how freeing that was? Yes! That was it! I pondered how that felt to me. I felt disrespected, patronized, and controlled. Wow! I need to honor when people say no, whether I agree with them or not. You see, when people won't honor your desire and you honor their no, you set them free. You can set yourself free also.

Freedom to choose

I spent years being a mistress, always the yes girl, to my husband. His first love is "projects"; namely the yard. In one case his job had taken him abroad for several weeks. He returned home on a Sunday afternoon and relaxed in front of the TV until bedtime. For the next *five days* he spent hours "putzing" in the yard (his words, not mine). We had not had any reconnect time. Friday afternoon came, and being slightly convicted, he says, "I just have *one* shutter to repair and I will be right in."

I showered, put on my "just-for-him" and waited…and waited…and waited. An hour and a half later, I donned my robe and walked out to see if he had fallen off of the ladder. There he was, shutter long done, plucking dandelions. Yes, plucking dandelions! To be honest with you, I was devastated. I felt so rejected. When he turned and saw me, his face dropped. I turned around, went into the house, took off my "for-him-only" and put my sweats on; the ugliest ones I could find. (This would be known as passive aggressive—the desire to "get" someone in a "non-getting" way.) But God! I gave my hurt to the Lord and He gave me His heart for my husband. I decided that even if he was a "won't," I could be a "would." I would forgive him and honor his no. The consequence of his "no" was my sweats.

Please be mindful that many, many times your husband's "won't" may really be a "can't." If you love him and desire to understand him, you must be in constant contact with the Spirit in this area. Ask the Holy Spirit to reveal your husband's heart to you. I mean that; right now. Get that paper. Say, "Holy Spirit, show me my husband's heart. Help me to understand him and see him as You do." Now wait; and write down things you see, feel, or sense. Look for them and continue to write them down. Good girl! When you know someone's heart, you *can* draw near to them, even in their "won'ts."

I had a horrible misperception in this area. My husband and I were having a very intense talk about our marriage. We had worked so hard and gone to such painful places for so long. Then one day he just says, "I don't know if I want to work on this anymore." Of course I immediately took that down the old "he does not want to be with me anymore and he hates his family" road. When I got over that, the Lord interpreted for me, "Jamie, what he is really saying, is, 'I don't know *how* to fix this. I am *afraid* to continue to fail you'." I *chose* to disregard *what* my husband said and to receive into my spirit God's truth: my husband just does not know how. I can forgive that. How could he know how without the guidance of the Spirit? My point: his "won't" may really be a "can't." Please don't miss that, sister.

I just lost over 200 pounds. Oh, yes I did! Let me tell you a story about that. Remember earlier when I said this has been a long and arduous journey? Well, just recently I believe I came to the end of this road. Praise God. As I was reading my years and years of journals preparing for this book, I came across a very disturbing pattern. I will go into greater depth about this subject in chapter 7, "Give Your Whole Heart." The pattern was one of asking and asking and asking God to help my husband to "grow in the Lord." That evening I gently shared with my husband of my discovery. He took in the information and then looked at me. "Jamie," he ventured, "I have been on the fence about my walk with God for twenty years. Maybe I just don't want to grow in the Lord."

My heart broke for him. "Oh, that he would desire and know You, Lord." The truth in the open, he asks me, "Do you respect me less now?" I lovingly replied, "Honey, I am so sad for you. But I actually respect you more. I have known for years that you really don't desire the things of the Lord. Now you are just being honest about it. Thank you!" The next day, free from *my* expectation of his growth in the Lord, he quit Bible study; he chose.

Oh, praise God for freedom; freedom to choose Him—or not; freedom to let go and release my husband *fully* unto the Lord. I got it! I *finally* got it: I must honor my husband's no and allow him to suffer his own consequences. Whew! I let go of my husband. That is 200 pounds I don't want to pick up again. Yippee!

So what about your "no"? When God calls us to do something, we do not have the option of being a "can't." When He calls us to do something, He gives us the ability to do it.

The "S" word

I am now going to talk about the "S" word. Yep, we are going to talk about godly submission. I put this in this chapter because I myself have told God that I *can't* do this. He resounded, "You *must*." So then I went into the "yeah, buts." I had a pastor call this being a billy goat Christian: "Yeah, but..." "Yeah, but, Lord, he doesn't follow You." "Yeah, but, Lord, I wasn't shown an example of this." "Yeah, but, Lord, he doesn't *deserve* to be submitted to." Bill E. Goat!

We all know the Word commands us to submit to our husbands as head of the household (Eph. 5:22–24). It is a difficult task to find a sweet, balanced teaching on this; so I am going to give you an example so you have an "earthly" picture of what this can look like for you and your spouse.

Before I go into my story, I need to press you a little bit. If the hair on the back of your neck stands up when I use the "S" word, I would like you to really understand your reaction. Do you have a job outside of the home? If you do, take a moment and think about your boss. Think about his or her position. Let's assume he or she does a good job. You feel valued and well trained by this person; in fact you appreciate when they give you pointers to grow in your position. But, what if your company sent out a memo: "We are pink slipping all department heads and are asking the lay people to run the business. If there is an area of disagreement on how to run things, you will have to do rock-paper-scissors"? Think about how that would work.

Have you ever been in a Bible study? Do you find it refreshing when the "leader" is well prepared, covers your group in prayer, and is ready to serve? I have; what a blessing! On the other hand, have you been in a study where the "leader" is not prepared, does not seek the Lord for the group, and is most interested in his or her position? Bummer! Why do we have a president of our country? Because we *desire* leadership. Do you get that? We know, in any other venue, that to have order we must have someone who is the leader. In fact, we pursue, hire, vote in, and train people to be leaders.

Now, let's ask ourselves why that makes so much sense out in the world but we won't embrace that in our own homes. Are you asking? Ask yourself why. Ask the Lord to show you why you may have a wrong perception of leadership in the home. In a precious marriage relationship, the leader of your home is in love with you. Why are we afraid of that?

I believe you need that story. Let me help you.

Karen and Toby were different in *every* way, except that Karen was a perfectionist, ordered and serious, while Toby was laid back, chaotic, and hilarious. And they were both committed to Jesus. In their zeal to know this Jesus, they opened themselves up to much balanced teaching about leadership and submission. They had been walking in it for about ten years when I met them. I was new to the Lord so I was "watching" them closely. When they had a difference of opinion, this couple came together and took it before the Lord. I was and am still blessed by watching the balance in their lives in this area.

Karen and Toby were cattle farmers, so they were also business partners. A precious example I saw played out something like this time and time again. Karen had been raised on a farm and was very knowledgeable about every aspect of running a farm. Toby was "learning." On this particular day, Karen found a great buy on a new bull. This bull was big, strong, and handsome and exactly what they had been asking God for in prayer. Karen called Toby in to look at the fine specimen on the Internet.

Excitedly she reported, "Honey! This is just what we have been praying for. In fact it is better than what I thought we would find. Isn't God good?" Toby peered over her shoulder at the image on the computer, agreed it was a beauty and a steal, and walked away. "Toby!" Karen yelled after him, incredulous at his lack of action. "We need to make a bid on this bull before it is gone."

Now remember, Karen had much more experience in this and *knew*, indeed, that they very easily could lose this bull if they did not act quickly. You see, she was *right*. "I know," Toby peacefully responded. Toby went to the barn. Karen was in the house pacing back and forth in prayer. She was "telling Jesus" on him. "Now, Lord, you know this is a good buy. We need this bull to expand our herd; and even though we have to travel 250 miles one way for him, he is perfect. Please reveal to Toby we need to buy this. But Lord, if I am wrong, I know you will also show Toby a different way." Then, she *let it go*. She trusted her Father to speak to her husband on the issue. With peace in her heart once again, she grabbed two cups of coffee and headed to the barn. It was there she found Toby. Her husband was on his knees, in the straw, seeking the Lord about the purchase.

Tears in her eyes, she recounted to me later how she was so blessed to see her husband before the

Lord on behalf of their business and humbled and repentant at her own anxiousness in the whole thing. "Jamie, I just love how the Lord is head over us and I can trust Him implicitly," she shared. They did *not* buy the bull that day. Toby had a very clear sense they should wait, so they did. Three days later they purchased a better bull at a better price only fifty miles away. Karen and Toby both had all the information, and they both sought the Lord. When Karen wanted to go forward with the first purchase and Toby did not, she acquiesced. Karen acquiesced to the Lord.

When we are able to get into our spirits we do not just submit to our husbands, we can embrace submitting to them. We know as we pray over them and for their leadership in our homes, God will be faithful and just to answer them and show them the perfect way for us as a family. As we learn to speak the truth in love to one another, we can share exactly how we feel in any situation. In fact we are to be our husband's help. The input he gets from you is invaluable. When we have a huge chasm between each other with an issue, it is time for both of us to hit our knees. If you are with an unbeliever, *you* will hit your knees. We can allow our husbands to make what we feel is a *wrong* choice because we know our Lord is faithful and will work through all things—even a wrong decision.

Toby, over the years, has developed a policy of sorts. If he and Karen do not agree on an issue, then he waits. He will spend more time seeking the Lord, asking if he has "missed it," and will bring the discussion to the table as many times as it takes until they are in unity or he knows that he *knows* which direction *they* should go. You see, precious sisters, just as God is for us, so is your husband for you.

Why then, can we submit in any other venue to a boss or leader (they may not even have your best interest at heart) but we will not do the same for our life partner? Silly, huh? Can I throw out a speculation? We will submit to a boss because there is something in it for us—$$. The truth of the Word is if we submit to our husbands as head of the home, there is great reward: you have obeyed your heavenly Father, blessed your children by honoring their daddy, and fanned a romantic flame in your marriage. Why, why, why can't we get this? Or, won't we? It might be the enemy, it might be others, or it just might be you. Go ask Him.

If this picture still leaves you struggling with the concept of submission, maybe this will help. Think of the last time your mother or mother-in-law came to visit. Did she tell you how to keep house? Maybe she rearranged your furniture. Maybe she made snide comments about your children's behavior. Wouldn't you be so blessed if she just came to visit and fit right into *your* schedule or asked you the best way she could ease your day? What if she was full of encouragement and praise? What a different picture, huh? Are you a big yes to that picture? Does that make sense? When she comes to *your* home, she should be in submission to the way you run your home. Not because you are over her but because it is the correct order—your house, your rules. This makes the atmosphere one of unity and peace because someone is in charge.

> Acknowledge the God of your father, and serve him with wholehearted devotion and with a willing mind, for the *Lord searches every heart and understands every motive behind the thoughts.*
> —1 CHRONICLES 28:9, EMPHASIS ADDED

Chapter 3

BROKEN LIKE A BRICK

PASTOR WITNESSED MY conversion from its infancy. In awe how God always had a message just for me in pastor's teachings, I shared jubilantly with him, "Pastor! It is such a coincidence that everything you talk about speaks directly to me!" (I was thinking he would certainly be honored at my thinking so highly of his teachings.) He grinned at me and said, "Well, Jamie, it's because you are such a big target!" It was then that I realized that pastor and everyone else "knew" that I needed a total redo. I guess I hadn't gotten the memo. I had a moment of self-realization.

I purposed in my heart from that day on to let my church body help me grow and change in the Lord. I so desired to be different—Christian, godly. I hadn't known I was a sinner until that time. My understanding of a "Christian" was "Jesus loves me this I know, for the Bible tells me so." Amen. Done deal. *My* "Jesus" had very little to do with my response to Him; the song said it, so it was.

UNEQUALLY YOKED

So my dialogue in my head went a little like this: "OK, fine then. I have been walking with the Lord for a while now; I have been in the Word, and have been going to Bible studies, home groups, and prayer groups. I have certainly learned a lot about myself, and I am so grateful God saved me when He did. I just can't understand why in the world God wouldn't change my husband. After all, it is definitely a godly request, right? And he *should* be the spiritual head of our home, so I just wish I knew what the problem is. OK, God, I am sick of living in a divided home and I don't even like him much less anything else. I really need to talk with my pastor."

The thoughts raced through my head as I headed for my appointment. Sometimes I wonder what Jesus is doing during these "conversations" with my poor little self. Is He shaking His head, laughing hysterically, or weeping? Now that I think about it, probably a little of each. So I go on: "This is going to be such a God thing. I know what the Bible says about being unequally yoked. All of that stuff about an unbelieving spouse is just confirmation of what *I* need to do. After I get my divorce, I can find a really awesome Christian man, have more kids, pray together, and raise our kids on fire for God. Pastor will confirm it for me, and I will be set free."

(I, of course, did not tell Pastor what this meeting was about because I am aware he prays about *everything*, so his answer will be godly and right.) "I will do exactly as he says because, God forbid, I would be disobedient to what God would want. Besides, I am really getting to love this 'godly counsel thing'; it has been so helpful to me."

It was a bright sunny day in late spring. I bounced into his office building already feeling a bit "set free." I had this picture in my head of moving my children and myself away from this unbeliever and onto a new life of love, happiness, and total Christianity.

The secretary welcomed me. Pastor was waiting for me in the office. He sat at his desk leaning back with hands folded in front of him. "Hi, Jamie, how are you doing today?" he inquired politely. "I'm doing pretty well," I responded truthfully, as I was anticipating the release of my "new life" to come at any moment. Then it happened; he tipped his chair forward, leaning toward me, his hands still folded, and looked me right in the eye. "Before we start today, I just want you to know; if you came here to ask me if it is OK to divorce Jim, it is *not* OK. God hates divorce."

I wish I could tell you the rest of our conversation. I cannot. His lips were moving but I was no longer "hearing." His words came crashing down on my parade. My float with my "new life" on it, me waving—elbow, elbow, wrist, wrist—was torn apart. This big black tornado came barreling down on my joyous procession. My Christian husband got sucked up in the funnel, my hot-for-God kids were Satanists, and my walk with God was a twisted tree with its leaves stripped off, naked and barren.

So, Pastor was saying, "Blah, blah, blah." I was numb. I looked at him, tears in my eyes, and quietly said, "OK"; and walked to my car...devastated. I pounded the steering wheel. I cried all the way home. Why, why, why do I have to stay with him? Why can I not be happy? Why do other women have husbands that love God? *Why?*

I spent a few days broken. (This is the part where Jesus weeps.) I was angry, disappointed, and, most of all, very lost. If I wasn't to have my "new life," then "What, Lord?" I really did desire to do what God told me, so I began to pray. I know the people around me and Pastor began to pray also. "God, help me!" I waited for the soft voice of the Lord to speak to me.

For the next few weeks I shared my sorrow with Christian friends. I began to hear the same scriptures and encouragements from many different people. I finally took in the realization that the Lord would have me to remain married. I was willing to obey that. I was well aware that I needed to start learning how this could possibly work.

I looked up all the scriptures I could find on husbands, as I *knew* God must have some pretty stern words of direction for them. I found them, all right. Using the word *husbands* for my reference, I found the scripture that was going to absolutely begin to change our marriage. I knew I would find one. I just didn't know it would be for *me*. The last part of Ephesians 5:33 says, "And the wife *must* respect her husband" (emphasis added).

Argh! I couldn't believe it! "*I* am the one that is following God and praying with my kids and taking them to church, and *I* have to respect *him*? For what?" My tirade went on for several moments as I had a heated discussion with the Lord. Imagine that. (This is the part where Jesus shakes His head.) I told Him all kinds of things I was sure He was *not* aware of or He would not ask me to do such a thing! "Respect what, God? He is mean, angry, domineering, controlling, a perfectionist, distant from us, unbelieving, spiteful, critical, selfish, and...well, he is cheap too."

Becoming willing

I had not yet, become "willing." I wept and shook my fist at God. As I poured out my heart, I felt a sense of quiet love come over me. It was a fond, "I know, dear," type feeling. I began to come to some level of rationale just knowing my God did indeed acknowledge this man was very difficult in many ways. He validated my pain, and that gave me the willingness. Besides just knowing the absolute importance of obeying my Father, I must also be willing. I had purposed in my heart before my meeting with Pastor to obey whatever God said through him. And now the Lord was showing me the way to go—respect.

Standing in my kitchen, tears streaming down my face, looking "past" the cathedral ceiling of my home and into the heavens, I surrendered. I said, "Lord, I will *not* lie. But if You show me one thing, just *one* thing I can *honestly* respect him for, I will do it out of love and obedience to You." The precious, still, small voice said to me, "He is a good provider." I fell to my knees and cried. My Savior began to show me something about this eighteen-year-old boy who had married me. He had sold his precious Mustang for a family car, worked more than one job at a time, and went to work without ever missing a day to a job he despised.

Repentance came quickly as the Lord continued to show me in my mind's eye the many times my husband came home absolutely exhausted. I never once acknowledged his hard work. God showed me the times he came in the door and I didn't see he had been degraded and discouraged. All he needed was hug or just a listening ear. I saw my husband being faithful to the penny with our finances and never having the satisfaction of "catching up." I never thanked him for being so wise with our so little money. I saw the headaches from the pressures and the stomachaches at the time of the sacred "profit number day." Yet, there I was in the picture with nothing. No words of encouragement. In fact, many times I let him know exactly what he needed to do differently and where he was going wrong. How sad. How very sad. I wept bitterly. I realized I did not know how to be a supportive wife. But I did know one thing, I was willing. "Please, God, I will respect him in this. Show me how to do it." And He did.

When the still small voice said, "Make chocolate chip cookies," I did. When my husband came in the door, I served the plate of cookies with a nice cold glass of milk. He wondered what the occasion was for such a treat. I humbled my pride and embarrassment. I let myself be kind and vulnerable before him. I looked him lovingly in the eye and said, "Because I appreciate how hard you work." There it was, out there in the open, a statement of respect and appreciation. His eyes tearing up, he said, "I think I'm going to cry. Thank you, honey." As I stood by this hardworking husband of mine devouring his treat, he wrapped his arm around my waist; attached, loving, intimate—just what I was longing for.

The saddest part of this story is what I am feeling right now, years later. I am weeping. When this took place, I had been married almost twelve years. I mourn over the years I did not respect my husband. My daughters were young at the time, very formative years not being taught to respect their Father. Apart from being my husband, this was a man—a man who was made in the image of his

Creator—being treated with disrespect and contempt in his own home. Oh, how sad.

My heart's cry is this will not be you. If it is, then know you have a redemptive God. You can ask the same question I did. Ask for just one area to respect your husband in and I know God will do it for you. And then be *willing* to obey the Word, repent, and humble yourself to be the wife God wants you to be no matter "where" your husband is. (This is the part where Jesus is laughing for joy.) He loves when we become willing.

I don't want you to ever be defeated because you think you have to be perfect in all the ways of the Lord all of the time. Honestly, I have been so strong in this area at times in my walk that the Lord was well pleased with me. I have also had times where I sunk back into periods of disrespect for my husband. I could tell you some of the circumstances surrounding those times; but now, on the other side of them, to do so would just be justifying my sinful behavior.

BROKENNESS

Have you ever been "broken"? Broken by a loving Father that sees what is in your future if you do not heed…quickly? I have. I will tell you, as painful as this is, it is life changing. Would I ever *choose* a quick, excruciating "breaking' over a long-term teaching? I don't know. I do know they are both necessary to grow in Christ. If you are not *sure* whether or not you have experienced a godly breaking, you haven't. Depending on how willing you are to heed one, they are usually an accelerated, magnified circumstance or struggle that nearly, for lack of a better word, *kills* you.

I remember once when I was "asking" the Lord to "break" whatever bondage my husband and I needed to get victory in our marriage. What I was desperately seeking was "breakthrough." The next day was absolute hell for Jim and me. We had a very small issue at hand. I chose to respond in a very ungodly way. I *never*—I repeat, *never*—call anyone, especially my husband, a swear word. Suddenly, I was a raging maniac. I understand now how people "snap." I certainly did that day. I was guilty of keeping anger and wounds stuffed deep within (under the guise of being "Christian"), and they certainly surfaced— in rage that day. Words came out of my mouth that I had not used since I had come to Christ. I called my husband a very vile name. He responded accordingly, and then left. I fell to my knees and cried out, "O my God, what just happened here!" I wept and wept. I was so grieved at the condition of my spirit. To behave like that, not only to my husband but also before the Lord, so grieved me.

Walls

My face in the carpet, I began to see a picture. It was Jesus. I was on one side of a brick wall and He was on the other side. All I could see was the top of His head. Then He knocked a brick down, then another. The jagged edges still showing, I looked at the wall. That is when He said, "You asked for breakthrough. You have to break through *before* you can walk through."

You see, the requirement is that *we* do the hard part first. We must allow the Lord to help us to break our walls down so we can then walk through them. I had to break through my sin. Ephesians 4:15 tells us to speak the truth in love. I had to break through my sin of not being totally open, truthful, and vulnerable with my hurts, angers, and frustrations. I "stuffed" them (in a very pious way) until they blew. I was broken, broken like a brick. Praise the Lord!

Walls do serve a purpose. They might keep you safe, keep someone out, or hide some hideous thing. I'm sure there are many purposes and uses for walls for each one of us.

Years ago, the Lord showed me how I had, unwittingly, used a wall in my own marriage. Jim and I had been going through a rich healing process. I was deeply involved in a small group, classes, prayer time, and personal ministry while Jim was regularly going to counseling for his anger issues. The Lord had given me much freedom in several areas. I was experiencing a *real* love for my husband for the first time in over twenty years. Keep in mind that I married at seventeen, for all of the wrong reasons.

We were at the phone company at our new location for his recent job change. We received our new phone number, and I proceeded to write it on the most available piece of paper. The paper ended up to be an important document that my husband needed for our next stop. Now I had written on it. When he saw what I had done, he turned to me and seethed, "Do you *know* what you just wrote on?" Of course I didn't. The women at the counter, witnessing this exchange, blushed with embarrassment. Refusing to cry in front of them, I turned around and walked out the door. I waited in the car for him. Tears burned my eyes. I was devastated, absolutely devastated!

I began to dialogue with myself. (Do you do this? Please tell me you do this.) Anyway, I am self talking: "What is wrong with me? It was no big deal. He has done way worse. O, my God! I am dying here; this hurts so badly! Why does this hurt so badly, Lord?" "He can hurt you now because you *love* him," the Lord whispered to me. "This is how it felt for your children because they *loved* their dad."

My husband is back in the car now. He takes my hand. "Jamie," he says. I cannot respond. He drives to a park to work this out. The pain is so overwhelming that I almost feel like my heart is truly breaking. I am now wrestling with two things. First, I will suffer pain now because I *love* him. The walls I had around my heart are down and this hurts really badly. I had kept those walls so high for so many years that his behavior didn't really affect me. How can someone hurt your heart if they can't reach it? "I don't know if I like this, Lord." And then I grieved for my babies. Those little girls who *wished* their daddy would play with them, who waited for him to approve of them, who *wanted* his love. "O, my God, I give You this pain." Through the tears, I explained to my husband what was happening in my heart. I told the *truth*, and we wept.

Surviving brokenness

I have been broken so many times that I feel like I should have a doctorate in it. Let me give you a couple hints for going through this precious process. If you can, always do it alone. You can go way deeper with the Lord when you are alone and, honestly, it gets ugly. Not only do I recommend alone, but far out in the country or at least with the windows closed and the air running. I have had some sounds come out of me in breakings that just might convince a neighbor to call 911.

Next, I like to use a towel. I'm not kidding! I call it my bawl towel. You see, tissues run out; they leave telltale white speckles around your nose, and you can go through a whole box in one breaking. Seriously.

This process always requires what I like to call "floor time." Floor time is lower than on your knees. Your knees kind of give the impression that you are still in a position of asking for something. The prone-flat-on-your-face position, hopefully, tells it all. When we "give up" the Lord is a happy Lord. Once, after one of these breakings, I yelled to the

Lord, "I give up!" "Good," He said. "When you have given up, that is when I will do miracles."

Have I been broken and broken and broken? Oh yeah, I have. I spent three days fasting and praying, asking the Lord to give me direction in my marriage or giving me an "out." I wrestled with the Lord on so many issues, I scoured the scriptures, and I even had friends stop by to pray over me. On day number three I was on the floor of my camper, with my towel and air conditioning on so the neighbors wouldn't hear me. I was spent before the Lord.

Again, after years of not even thinking about it, I was entertaining my life's plan after I got divorced. Here is how this ridiculous dialogue went. "Lord, if I am to get divorced, will You please just show me," I pleaded. Silence. Hours went by. "Please, Lord!" Silence. I felt His heavy presence, heavy in a not so good way. Days went by; I was still fasting and praying. It felt like a "we are *not* going to discuss this, young lady, it goes against My Word" type silence. Or like, "I refuse to enter into this conversation. You know better!" Yikes!

"Of course You are not going to give me the A-OK to get divorced, Lord. I will just have to decide what I think." As clear as a bell, I hear, "Jamie! Do you really *want* a divorce?" He repeats, "Do you *really want* a divorce?" And then my sweet Jesus gave me a vision. I see before me how my life would be as a divorced person. I see my kids at holiday times with a split family. I see the broken marriage covenant.

I see me having to go back to school at my ripe old age. I see my husband with someone else. I see not being able to travel to visit my kids because of money issues. I see... "No! No, Lord! I do *not* want a divorce. I really do not want to be divorced. I just want the pain to stop."

Oh what sweet release, ladies. The brokenness led me to the realization that I would do whatever it took to keep my marriage. I also understood it was going to have to be His way.

His Way

Then I found out what "His way" was.

My husband and I were attending my girlfriend's daughter's wedding. Her daughter and future son-in-law both loved the Lord, so watching that sweet pure union was even more special. The pastor goes to 1 Corinthians 13:4: "Love is patient"... nope, "love is kind"... nope, and on through the rest of the scripture. Sitting next to me is my husband, doing the same thing—nope, nope, and nope. In the car on the way home he asks me, "How did you feel about the sermon?" "It made me sick to my stomach to see how far down the pit we've gone," I return. Silence.

That night I asked him to sleep in the other room as I was very tired and he snores... loudly! I fell into the most precious sleep. I slept for about two hours and then began to wake. I was in that not-yet-quite-awake place. The strangest thing was happening. I felt like I was wrapped in bubble wrap. All of the bubbles had joy in them. It was the most beautiful feeling, wrapped in joy.

I fell back to sleep for about another two hours. When I awoke again, I was in a very dark place. My spirit was heavy within me. "Love is patient, love is kind." Over and over again those words kept rolling around in my spirit. I became more and more agitated and began to thrash in the bed. My body, spirit, and mind were wrestling. The words became louder and louder. "*Love is patient, love is kind!*" Then, "Are you *willing*, Jamie?"

I pictured my husband and all of the things he had promised to "work on." "He was a 'no' to all of them, Lord." I saw the things he says. "They are so hurtful and mean, Lord." I saw how long I'd been waiting for him to change. "He won't, Lord; he won't." Again, "Are you willing?" "No! Not only am I *not* willing, but I *hate* him, Lord!" There I said it. (I was seriously waiting to go straight to hell, do not pass Peter.) God knows already anyway, so I might as well just be honest, right? "I hate him and I am *not* willing; so now I'm going to hell. I don't want to go to hell; and I know You love him, Lord. I am so sorry."

Lying on my back, tears filling my ears, I am wrestling with my King. Then my precious Savior says, "Jamie, you don't hate him. You hate what he *has done* to you and your children." Do you know how blessed we are to have a King who knows us better than we know ourselves? Like, I had just totally *told*

Him that I needed to go to hell. Whew! Close one.
I am so glad I don't call the shots. Finally, an hour
and a half later, I am broken, broken like a brick,
the walls coming down. "Oh, thank You, Jesus, that
I don't hate him. I am free from that belief. I do not
hate him. Lord, I am willing. I surrender. *But*, if I
surrender, You have to *show me how* to do this. I do
not know what to do, Daddy. I *do not know* what I
can say or not say. This is all up to You now." Can't
you just hear the Lord? Big sigh, "Finally!" Then I
slept.

You just won't believe what happened next. The
next morning, while I was putting on my makeup,
my husband comes into the room. He sits down
on the bed and says, "Come here." He draws me in
between his legs so I am standing before him. Yes,
I am short enough that we are now face-to-face. He
wraps his arms around my waist and looks into my
eyes. Eyes moist with tears, he looks deeply into
mine; and, out of the blue, asks, "Do you *hate* me?"

I start to bawl! I am filled with thanksgiving. My
Father has gone before me and put this question on
my husband's heart. "You *heard* me, Lord, you *heard*
me!" Jeremiah 33:3 tells us: "Call to me and I will
answer you." I asked two things of the Lord the night
before. "I am willing Lord if you will *show me* how
to do this; and *what can I and can I not speak* to my
husband." Oh, He is faithful; He is faithful!

Remember the "bubbles of joy" I experienced the
first time I woke up? I know the Lord was showing

me that is what He has for me, *if* I am willing—joy, pure bubble wrapped joy.

He did it for me. And He will do it for you.

Pattern for marriage

Let me share the pattern in my marriage that I walk in that brings me to the end of me. This is what it almost always looks like. My sins are disobedience, resentment, and then unforgiveness. I've run around that mountain so many times that I have a private freeway with my name on it: "Jamie's Junkway: private; keep off." Really! So I go around and around and around. Ever heard the saying that insanity is doing the same thing over and over and expecting different results? Well, I want to tell you, sometimes I go *really fast* and leave a big old dust plume behind me. I can see Jesus trying to stop me. He has His hand out to help me, and I whiz by so fast His hair blows and His face gets pulled taut like Mach 4 or something. When I am doing this, He usually has to protect the people around me because I am so wild that I will just run them over and leave them dead in my wake. The engine that propels that baby sounds kind of like this: "I have to fix this; I can't live like this anymore; that's it, this stops now!" Running, running, running.

Then we have the other pattern; same issues, different pace. I am going around the mountain plodding, going, pulling, going, crawling. It seems I am almost at a standstill; the mountain remains and I have barely moved. And there is Jesus; this time He is walking next to me. When I stumble from the weight of my load, He begins to pick it up to carry it for me and I give Him a polite, "No thanks; got it under control." He honors me and lets go. He usually has to cover those around me because the weight of my "burden" leaves others with guilt that is not theirs to carry. The engine that propels this engine sounds a bit like this: "I will help him, convince him, change him, teach him, and preach him." Sheesh! Pulling, pulling, pulling.

At the end of each of these roads is the *exact* same destination: disobedience, resentment, and unforgiveness.

How do I get to the end of this road—the end of me and the weight of my sin? Through Him and His heavy hand. Job 36:10 tells us, "He makes them listen to correction and commands them to repent of their evil." Then in verse 13 we read, "The godless in heart harbor resentment: even when He fetters them, they do *not* cry for help" (emphasis added).

So I am on the floor, you guessed it, with my towel. I wrestle and wrestle with the Lord. I am *always* so tired when I finally get "done" going around the mountain. He reveals these scriptures to me, and I know it is time to repent. So, I do. I stand to thank Him for forgiving me; thank Him for breaking me; thank Him for rebuilding my walls with His walls of protection, guidance, and security. Blessed assurance, Jesus is mine.

Chapter 4

EMASCULATE

*I*SN'T IT FUNNY how you don't know the things that you do or don't do until someone shows you a different way?

In our younger years Michelle and I had played softball, partied, cussed, and chased around together. We were puny but punchy. Most might have considered us the "bad girls" on the team. Then I came to Christ. We were still friends but our relationship was different. I was "chasing" Him now. I had been walking with the Lord for a couple of years when she came to me and said, "Jamie, I was watching a Christian TV program and he was saying all the stuff you have said since you've 'changed.' I really need to learn more about the Lord." I was thrilled.

Long story short, after that conversation with Michelle, the Lord had me lead a women's Bible study. In my youthful ignorance, the Lord used me to usher several woman to Him, including Michelle. My advice to you is, be careful who you bring to the Lord because they just might—OK, they *will*—be used to move, stretch, and grow you.

Words We Say

About a year after her full-blown come-to-Jesus conversion, Michelle knocks on my door. Looking down from the top of my split foyer landing, I "see" it. Yep, there is that "look." Michelle has a prophetic vision gifting in the Lord. I have watched this gift in her grow and be used in some powerful ways. When she has a "word," she gets this wild looking-past-you face. Today I *know* "it" is coming my way. I am so excited, pretty sure she's going have a word about my calling or a blessing or some strong direction from the Lord about my walk with Him.

She doesn't even sit down. "I have to say something to you," she forces out. I am beginning to sense the foreboding in her. I'm thinking how cute it is that she is struggling with getting the word out. But I understand how one struggles with fear and doubt when giving a "mentor" a word—poor thing. "Michelle," I say, "If you have something from the Lord for me, I need to hear it no matter what it is." "OK," she sighs, sucks in her breath, and blurts, "When you talk to Jim the way you do..." (There is a long pause; her wild eyes are looking away from me, her fists in a ball.) Then quickly she says, "...it's just like you are cutting off his [manhood]. I gotta go to work." She turns around and *runs* out the door.

I am still at the top of the landing, standing, looking down the now empty foyer. Did this just happen? "Really, Lord?" Well, I think, trying to soak in what she said, "Well, yeah, but Jim's so... He doesn't... He won't... He should... Oh no! Are You talking about the scripture that says I need to treat my husband with respect? You want me to speak respectfully no matter how he is?" (Eph. 5:33).

When I was finished with all of my arguing, the Lord began to show me the ways, words, and attitudes I used against my husband. I bawl like a little girl. Anyway, I scan over my childhood for examples of how a wife "should" speak to her husband. I can't find any! "Lord, I can't find *any*!"

Now, I am not saying there was no one in my life who honored her husband. I am saying it must have been few enough that I really couldn't recall anyone as an example. In all honesty, the women in my life were either very biting to the men in their lives or very reserved, not saying much at all—neither kind nor demeaning.

Face down on the floor, snot running into my bawl-baby towel, I cry out to my Daddy. "Lord, I don't know how! I honestly don't know *how* to talk 'nice' to my husband." Then I cry more. I wonder what the Lord is doing while He waits for these "sessions" that I have with myself to be done. I don't know, but I am a bit embarrassed at the thought of it. So, I'm finished. (You will know this when you can't cry anymore and your hiccupping and your own voice is beginning to aggravate you.) And He speaks and shows me. I see my husband. I see me. I see me saying to my husband, "Thank you, I appreciate that. I would love to do that for you. No problem, how can I help you?" Wow! These are words that I say often to *others*. Ouch!. Jezzy-Jamie is in the room. But my Jesus shows me *how* to talk to Jim.

Let's look at Ms. Jezebel's words to her husband in 1 Kings 21:7. Ahab was basically in a funk. He had "asked" Naboth to hand over his vineyard (v. 2). As king, Ahab figured he could just confiscate it; but covenantal law forbade him to do so. Naboth pretty much said no (v. 3). So Ahab (in true "no action" spirit) went home and pouted (v. 4). We see a clear example of the Ahab spirit at work here in the king. By contrast, Naboth had a true leader-man spirit and he stood for what was rightfully his.

So, Ahab is pouting, angry, not eating, and actually in bed. Ms. Jezebel "came in and asked him" (v. 5). Really? Let's look at her personality. Ms. kills-those-in-her-path probably didn't just come in and ask him. I would venture that she *stormed* into his chambers and screamed at him (my interpretation in brackets), "Is this how you act as king over Israel [you puny little powerless man]? Get up and eat [big baby]! Cheer up. I'll get you the vineyard of Naboth the Jezreelite [I'll usurp your authority, control your deal, and show you how to be a man]" (v. 7). When Jezebel is done cutting off her own husband at the knees with her words, she proceeds to go out and do *his* work *her* way, sealing his false belief that she is stronger and more capable than he is. Jezebel perverts the "created helper" in us to a "manufactured manipulator."

You see, ladies, we have the power to make or break our husbands. Genesis 2:18 says that we were created to be our husband's *helper*. Put the stones down, ladies! I did not say that; the Word does. Does a helper build up or tear down, encourage or discourage, rail or rally? Our ways, words, and attitudes towards our husbands *are* our ministry unto Christ. Proverbs 14:1 says that "the wise woman *builds* her house [up], but with her own hands [mouth] the foolish woman *tears* hers *down*" (emphasis added). Is that you? I know it has been me. Don't we have enough things in our marriages that are trying to tear our homes apart without our tongue helping to destroy that very thing we are so desperately trying to hold together?

Maybe you would prefer someone else be that helper for your husband? Really? I'm going to tell you what that might look like. She might be really pretty, younger, tighter, taller, tinier, sassier, sillier, quieter, or just "there." What I do know for sure is that you will be very surprised at what attracts him. She possesses something you do not, if you struggle with emasculating your husband with your words. I have seen this time and time again. A man leaves his wife for a very *not* good-looking gal. Everyone tries to figure out what he "sees" in her. And then you meet her. She is pleasant, kind, and, yes, encouraging to him. She is beautiful to him. She has embraced her "created" role.

I had a small picture of this in my world one day. As my walk grew, I began to develop friendships with women who loved Jesus. This day, one of these friends, Stephanie, popped by for some coffee, chocolate, and fellowship—lots of each. I was pretty much like a sponge soaking up all I could about living for and walking with the Lord. Stephanie had a pure heart. She loved the Lord more than anyone I had ever met, was a seeker of His face, and doer of the Word. I admired her and, to this day, consider her the "discipler" of my faith.

We were just finishing a great time of fellowship when my husband arrived home from work. As he came up the stairs, it seemed I was watching a slow motion movie. My eyes on Stephanie, I watch her turn her head towards Jim. I watch as she turns her body toward him—wide grin, open heart, smiling eyes—and greets him. "Hi, Jim!" she almost squeals. He snaps his head in her direction, surprised by the greeting, unlike what he usually gets—if I am in the room, that is. Usually indifference, instruction for repairs, or a gripe might meet him. She very innocently and sweetly *asks* about his day, *listens* to him, and then *validates* him with, "You really deal with a lot of different scenarios don't you?" Her interest in *him* and *his* day has opened him like I have never seen. My husband's countenance has soared, his voice is strengthened, and he is sharing—yeah, sharing—with enthusiasm.

Snap! Snap! Snap! Just like a photo shoot, the Lord shows me frame by frame the *power* this woman had over *my* husband. Ladies, this encounter was as innocent, pure, and loving in Jesus as can be. But the Lord showed me just how easy it would be for an "evil" woman to "steal" my man—with just words. He showed me the power I have to build him up or tear him down. I decided that day *I* would be the one who changed my husband's countenance, not another.

MANIPULATION

Sometimes the Lord just lets me observe other Jezzys. On this particular day I was attending the wedding of one of my close friend's daughter. The wedding was being held out of town, so many of us had traveled long distances and rented rooms for the evening. I scanned the room for familiar faces. Merit was across the room. As always, she was engaging, joyous, and encouraging. Encouragement was one of the gifts the Lord had blessed her mightily with. She was seated with people from our home church. They were in absolute uproarious laughter over some story she was sharing. I had moved from the area a couple years earlier so was very much excited to reconnect with this group. The Lord had something different for me that day.

I grabbed a seat next to Merit. We all shared our condensed versions of family updates and then each began to go one way or another; one to the dance floor, one to the chocolate bar, another to mingle here or there. I was surprised Merit was able to attend, as I knew she was unemployed, in mounting credit card debt, and struggling financially with two children to provide for. She was in her third year of separation from her husband. She was praying and waiting for restoration of her marriage. I excitedly proclaimed, "Merit! I am so glad you were able to be here! Where are the girls?" She clapped her hands together, scrunched her shoulders in glee, and giggled. Then she says, "Jamie, you won't believe it!" She was right; I wouldn't.

Maybe it was because I had been removed for a couple years so I was seeing with clearer vision, or maybe it was that my Jesus gave me His view that day, or maybe both. "It" unfolded. "Well," she leans in, looks around as if in a covert operation, and proceeds to spin the tale (again, my interpretation is in brackets): "I got an invite for the wedding and I knew I couldn't afford to go [poor Merit]. The *girls* were so disappointed [I will manipulate anything to get what I want] and I really wanted to go [no matter what]. I just *knew* the 'Lord' [or my husband I am separated from] would make a way for us to go [because I am religious]."

I am listening to how the "Lord" worked this out. She continues: "So I called Kyle [her husband she is separated from], told him about the wedding, and *suggested* we go as a *family* [because Kyle must be desperate to be by his wife and kids]. He was concerned he wasn't invited [which he wasn't] but I assured him [lied] they would *love* to have him. You know how egotistical he is. I knew he would fall for that."

My heart began to sink: "Am I seeing what I think I am seeing, Lord?" She looks around again. Now I know she really doesn't want people to hear this story. She goes on, "So, tee-hee, I convince him not only to *come with* and *drive* us, but to get a room for him and the girls *and* a separate one for me since we *are* separated." She is clapping; I am feeling sick. "And get this! When he picked us up and saw the clothes the girls had on, he took us directly to the mall for new dresses for them for tonight. Ha-ha! And now he has them in the pool and then off to bed because I told him that they were *really* missing him and need time with *just him*. So, I have the whole night free!"

She is roaring now and rocking in her chair in hysterics. Right when I think I am going to vomit, she finishes the diatribe with the final blow. Leaning in and looking around again, she whispers, "The sad part is, Jamie, no one here has even *talked* to him. I can't believe he bought into they would *want* to see him." Manipulator! What God *created* as helper, we have *manufactured* into a "man-ipulator." I got up.

I went to find him. I wanted to tell him how glad I was to see him and what a good dad he was. He was gone in his room with his daughters.

That day I was ashamed of my sister, ashamed of me, and ashamed of us—the sisterhood of manipulators. You know who you are, and I know when I have done it. "Dear God, forgive us!"

Do you know the description of the word *perverted*? It is deviating greatly from what is considered right and correct. My Christian sister had perverted every part of her relationship with this man, leaving him powerless. He had been told he didn't know how to parent, didn't know how to run his business, didn't know how to manage finances, didn't know how to be a Christian, and on and on. He came to believe that and receive it in his spirit. She manipulated his emotions, his position of leadership in his family, and his finances, among other things. She had destroyed the man and the very marriage that she was trying to hold on to.

There is a good example of this in the story of Jezebel and Elijah the prophet of the Lord found in 1 Kings 19:1–5. Jezebel perverted everything about her husband's kingship, manipulated outcomes, and brought this great prophet to utter dismay. Elijah not only told the Lord he had had enough, but he prayed that he might die (v. 4).

Our husbands want to be the head of the house (even our Ahab brothers). Sometimes they do not know how, and other times the Jezzy in their life has stripped them of their position. How many times have you said to your husband, "You are not even the leader of our home"? I know I have. I also know that is a lie. You see, the Bible says your husband *is* the head of the house. (See 1 Corinthians 11:3; Ephesians 5:23; Genesis 3:16.) It is not just a suggestion.

Are you beginning to see a pattern here? Are you really believing the Word is the truth or not? Some of us have even accused our husbands of keeping us from our ministry because *they* are not godly enough. What a heavy thing to put on another human being, much less being bold enough to basically say out loud, "Well, I would be in ministry but God isn't big enough to do that because of my husband." Oops.

Once, in a "discussion" with my husband, I was informing him if he was "serious" about a certain issue in his life he would be responding in a different way. It went kind of like this: "Jim, I am very frustrated at your lack of dealing with this issue in your life. A man desperate for change would... Blah, blah, blah." My husband, incredulous, retorts, "I don't even get to decide how I should react? Who are you to tell me an appropriate response to a struggle? Jamie! I am *not you!*" My "word" from Michelle floated in the back of my mind.

It is a funny thing how women desperately try to train their men to be more like them. Then when they are more like us, we don't like that they are not more of a man. What a powerful way to rob some-one's masculinity: tell them they need to be more like a woman. Wow! My eyes wide open, I "got" it. He was right. Who *am* I that I "know" how he should be. His Creator knows him perfectly. I don't. In fact, I realize I have no clue how it is to be him.

SEXUALITY

Jezebel, following the Baal she worshiped, knew the power she possessed in her sexuality. The worship of Baal included orgies, prostitution, and seduction. Second Kings 9:30 says, "When Jezebel heard about it, she painted her eyes, arranged her hair and looked out of a window." Can we assume her motive was seduction? Hanging out the window in that day was inappropriate at best. We know that she was a manipulator and a controller and possibly a harlot too. If you have ever been in a foreign country and even some cities here, you can see women painted up, hair all done up, and hanging out of windows. It is pretty apparent what they are looking for—most likely *not* a taxi. The point is, we *know* the power we have in sex. We can build up or tear down with it.

Personally, this is not an area I struggled with in my marriage. Very few times have said no to my husband, for whatever reason. In the worst of our relationship, I was able to surrender myself to my husband sexually just because the Lord tells me to. I confess there were times I cried and times that I did not enjoy it.

Manipulation by deprivation

First Corinthian 7:5 says, "Do *not* deprive each other except by mutual consent and for a time, so that you may devote yourselves to prayer. Then come together again so that Satan will *not* tempt you because of your lack of self-control" (emphasis added). Really? Yeah, really. I am not going into a deep theological teaching about this. I am going to address the way that we render our husbands powerless when we use sex as a tool in a negative, ungodly way.

We are *all* guilty of using seduction, especially in our premarriage relationships. Come on now, can you truly tell me you didn't at least put on your most appealing outfit or used a little more make up to allure him? Yeah, the lust of the eyes (1 John 2:16). We knew he was looking! We *know* how to seduce.

Now don't get me wrong. Seduction in *marriage* is not only allowed, it is *needed*. Oh, I need to say that again: seduction in marriage is not only allowed, it is needed. When we seduce our husbands, it makes him feel like a man. Ladies, remember my friend who raised my husband's countenance? Well, there are women out there that will be more than happy.... You know what I mean!

Do I think you should seduce him out of fear that he will look elsewhere? Absolutely not! I am saying that you possess a precious gift—your body—and you can present it to him and bless him with it. Or, you can keep it under those nasty sweats and rob him. You choose. If you think I am talking about wearing some ridiculous outfit, not necessarily. I *am* talking about dressing and looking the way that pleases *him*, makes him happy. You need to do it for him. It is not about you.

He won't even care if your lumps and bumps are not all in the right places anymore. Your husband thinks you are sexy because you are *his*. That, in itself, is sexy to him. It is sexy to men to know they have sex available with their wives at all times. "Yep, hunted her, bagged her, and now she's mine, mine, mine!" Don't believe me? It's just like a hunter or fisherman that gets his "game" and has it stuffed so they can look at it and pet it. He loves you, wants you, and needs to touch you. It brings him great pleasure. If you really don't want to do it for him, do it for *Him*. Yeah, you can even say, "Lord, I'm going to [insert your husband's special thing] just in obedience to You, for the purpose of blessing my husband." He will say, "Way to go, sweetheart!"

There is no debate. Not giving of yourself is sin. One of the worst kinds of withholding sex that takes place is the kind that is fueled by revenge: "He hurt me so I'm not going to..." Revenge is sin. Stop it! Or, how about pout withholding? That is the one that shuts down sex when you don't get your way. Oh, I love this one: "Our relationship is really hard right now, so I don't *feel* like it." Wow! If I withheld sex every time my marriage was in trouble, I might be childless. Or, how about "I'm tired," "I have a headache," "My favorite TV show is on right now,"

"I got barfed on four times today," or whatever else your "withholding" might be about.

Will you look at that with the Lord? Ask some questions: "Why do I withhold, Lord?" "When do I withhold, Lord?" "What is my heart when I withhold, Lord?" "Do I use sex to get my way, Lord?" "Do I need to be more open about what I like or dislike sexually, Lord?" Are you asking Him? Ask now; really, *now*.

Go back with me to the second part of the scripture: "Come together again so that Satan will not tempt you" (1 Cor. 7:5). Isn't this precious? God Himself is giving us a warning: "Make sure you have sex, or infidelity might happen." It's loud and clear, ladies. When we are apart sexually, it *weakens* our husbands. Is that really what you want, a weak husband? I know you don't. So many women complain to me about their "weak" husbands but are not willing to look at the areas *they* have contributed to that weakness. Are you able to see the big picture?

Manipulation by seduction

The other side of that coin is the woman who uses sex to get her way. Instead of withholding, she uses sexual acts, sexual words, and promises of sexual things to get material things or even certain decisions to go her way. We now can see Jezzy in full swing. She sets her eyes on what she wants, makes a plan to get it, and follows through with the seduction. She has deceived herself that this will bring her success. All the while she is manipulating and controlling the circumstance, her husband is deceived into thinking she really desires him. Ugly picture, huh?

So here is what really happens. She uses seduction for control, belittling herself and the intimate act of sex. He then, under the spirit of seduction, makes a decision *not* out of wisdom but out of lust. Ultimately she has created an atmosphere where her husband may have made a wrong decision devoid of wisdom that can have lasting negative ramifications on both of them. Her "success" may have put them in horrible debt, emotional strife, or even out of God's will. Simply put, don't "sex" your husband into a new car, house, outfit, behavior, or event. Let him make decisions in wisdom, with the Lord.

Humble yourself

Some of us high-end Jezzys "think" we know stuff. Do you understand that the King of the universe has created us male and female? This means we are *very* different. Will you die to the fact that you do not understand his sexuality? Humble yourself to ask your husband how it is for him. Knowledge is power, ladies.

Let me help you a little. It might look like this when you have your "sex" talk with your husband. "Honey, when I turn you down sexually, how does it feel emotionally, physically and mentally?" Listen to him. Listen with a pure, honest heart. "Listen" means *be quiet*. When he says, "I am in physical pain when I need sex," you may *not* roll your eyes, quote a scripture about dying to flesh, or remind him of the pain of childbirth. Not nice, ladies! Do you *hear* him? Can you receive into your spirit the man you say you adore is in physical pain? *You* are the answer to that longing, ladies. What an honor!

Will you laugh at him if he tells you he feels rejected when you turn him down? (After all, how many times has he rejected you in one way or another?) Yes, Jezzy would choose to tell him that. Unless you are loaded with testosterone, you will not "get" when he needs that release—he can't think clearly, has a harder time reigning in anger and frustration, and he feels aggressive. Built up testosterone is like a powder keg; and *you* hold the key to alleviate that in his life. Now that is what I call power! In my eyes, to *not* provide that relief for your husband is counterproductive. I want my husband to be clear minded, effective, and ambitious in his day. I am on *his* side.

Other Ways to Emasculate

Where have you emasculated your husband? It may not be in one of the aforementioned areas. Ask the Lord where it is for you. I can tell you some of my areas are *not* pretty. Some of them are from long ago and I have had victory over them since, but I'm still going to share them. I am going to mention them, put them right out there, and let the Lord use my garbage for good. OK?

Early in my marriage (I will use the excuse that I did not know Jesus then) I was on a warpath. The people in the middle of that path were my in-laws; poor things. Pointing out his parents' faults allowed me to "show" my husband his "crazy ways" without *directly* accusing him. How's that for being devious and manipulating? I am wondering now why I thought I was in charge of that anyway. This behavior, again, is very counterproductive. What do you really think you are going to gain by telling your mate that the people he loves the most (after you) stink? Really? Imagine how blessed and lifted up he would be if you honor them. I know now that the only thing that was really was going on was that I did not know how to "accept one another, then, just as Christ accepted you, in order to bring praise to God" (Rom. 15:7).

Or, how many times did I sit in the car seething because my husband likes to drive *under* the speed limit on a long trip? I take a book now.

Did I render my husband useless in parenting by constantly telling him he didn't know how to parent? We are still repairing that mess and our children are grown with children of their own. You see, ladies, when you tell someone "you can't, you can't, you can't," eventually they *don't*.

Quoting scriptures at someone is never effective when they are not interested, have no understanding, or *are* talking to God themselves. I would assume that it makes them feel like they are in kindergarten or just not able to "understand" the Word like you. My husband has on occasion stopped me and reminded me to *stop*.

I can't leave out the insidious nagging. Remember, we are talking about emasculating. I am well aware that often a wife will nag because it *seems* her husband won't respond. Ladies, he *has* responded; his answer is no. If he is unable or unwilling to heed, you must go back to the Lord and ask Him how *you* should respond. We are accountable to God how *we* are, not how our husband is. If you do not know how to respond in a balanced, godly way, you need to seek a mentor or counselor or get a book on communication. Nagging can be so easily replaced with, "Honey, I am really frustrated that the broken door has not been fixed. Can we pick a date it will be done by? Or, if you don't have time or don't want to do it, I can help you find someone to hire to do that. What do you think?" Wow! You could even give him *grace* and tell him he can think about it for a day or two and get back to you. It is OK for you to want a time limit. You can give him the power back by letting him choose the timing. Ladies, give him back the power *to be a man*.

I have a favorite video that I have watched at least 100 times and taught from it several times called *The Bride*, done by a church in the south many years ago. At the end a white horse comes down the aisle, Jesus gets off and dances with His new bride, and then He picks her up and swings her around. (Are you kidding? I don't know about you, but it has been years since my husband has been able to pick me up.) I weep when I see this part—every time. God created your husband with the desire to be just that to you— your husband who can pick you up. I don't care what you think about that, it is true. Have you ever heard the saying, "If you treat him like a king, he will treat you like a queen?" Part of that, ladies, is *allowing* him to pick you up.

WORDS TO BUILD UP

I have a friend who is the best mother I have ever met. I tell her that all of the time. I am going to call her Heather. I have known her since her children were very small. I can only pray that one of my granddaughters meets and marries the kind of young men this friend is training up. One of my earliest recollections of how balanced she is happened when her youngest son was about two and one-half. She brought out a piece of paper for each of us to color on. I smiled at the wisdom in that. Us having paper and colors gave him the impression that we were "all" doing a project together. Little did he know it was a distraction for him so we could visit.

We started to "color," and this little guy proceeds to break his stack of crayons in half. She softly puts her hand on top of his and says, "Austin, if you choose to do that, your colors will be broken for next time." He looks at her and continues to break his colors. When he is finished he reaches his fat little fist across the table for her crayons. Heather puts her hand over them and says, "Son, I am sorry.

Your colors are right there and you chose to break them. Mommy is not sharing her colors because she wants hers to stay nice." Wow! What power! From just a toddler, this little boy is being spoken to in a respectful manner, touched kindly, allowed to make choices, and allowed to suffer the consequences of those choices.

Mommas, you have power to raise a *man*. The greatest thing Heather has exampled to her sons is their position in the home. She knows the Word and honors her husband as the head of their home. Her sons see the responsibility and power in that. My favorites are when I hear her ask Austin (who is six now), "Austin, can I feel your muscle today? Oh my, it is so much bigger than yesterday! You must have been working hard." Or, she asks her teenager, "Son [what an honorable way to address your young man], the groceries are heavy; would you please bring them in for me?" My very favorite is when she *speaks* into them, saying, "Son, God is going to use your gifts and talents in a mighty way some day." "Yeah," answers Nick (who is thirteen now), flipping his long hair to the side, "I know." He has such confidence; because his Mother knew the power of her words.

When these two boys come to her for advice or crying over an offense on the playground, she trusts *them* with the problem. "Well, how do you think you should respond, son?" she will inquire. Austin will talk it out and talk it out and talk it out. After about six scenarios he will come to his conclusion. It is usually right on and godly. Nick will stand there, mouth open, silent. For a minute you think he has gone into a standing coma; but no, he answers, "I guess I need to..." And he ends with a godly resolution to the situation. She responds to both the same way, "I *knew* that you knew what God would have you do. You are so smart, son." I am sure if I asked her she would tell me she is interceding the whole time in her head. My friend has figured out that she has the power to *build* these boys *up or tear* them *down.*

We have been talking about sons. Why would we be any different with our husbands? They are men. We need to speak strength, encouragement, power, success, and a myriad of positive life-giving things to them; and we *will* reap harvest. Over the years, I have watched as Heather has cultivated the ground and put good seed into her sons. I know she will reap an awesome harvest.

Arizona adventure

My husband and I go to Arizona every winter for a break from our bitter, long, torturous, evil (you get it) winters. On one visit I decided we would take a trip up to the Grand Canyon.

First, I have to give you a little back info on myself. At sixteen I "counseled" my parents to seek counseling instead of divorcing. I rode and broke my own horses. I stood up to a lesbian gym teacher who was watching girls shower. I fought an unfair landlord and won. I was married at seventeen and had three kids by the age of twenty-three; and I am still married today, thirty-seven years later. Get the picture? I'm no namby-pamby, OK?

Anyway, we drive up to the Grand Canyon. (If you've never been, go. It is a present from the Lord for your eyes and spirit. His majesty is revealed in a magnificent way.) We get out of the car and there is a holy hush. Neither one of us can speak. The beauty leaving us breathless, we just stand in silence. A little prickle goes up the back of my neck. I am well aware that I am not thrilled about heights, but I think I'm a little scared. We drive to the next lookout. It has a three-foot brick wall but no guardrails. Oh, I am definitely not liking this! My husband must see the look on my face. He says, "You OK?" "Yeah, I'm fine," I lie. I am looking at the tiny little woman that came off of the tour bus. She is standing on a jutting-out-over-the-canyon thing, bent over, her leg back, arms spread like Nancy Kerrigan doing whatever that is on the ice. Yikes! I am sweating now. Yep, scared!

"Should we go to one more lookout before it's time to go?" my husband asks excitedly. How can I say, "No, I'm too chicken; let's leave"? "Sure," I lie again. We get to the last lookout and it is at least a million miles out and only twelve inches wide (so, it is probably a hundred feet out, twenty feet wide, and has a guardrail—same thing). Jim takes my hand, and we begin to go out. I stop. He walks a few more feet, turns around, and says, "What's the matter?" I *almost* go into the "if you were in tune to me at *all*, you would know that I am so scared I am about to have a stroke" mode. But I didn't. I say, "I don't know what's wrong with me, but I am terrified right now." He puts his hand out (notice he didn't tell me I was being dumb). "Come on, honey. Take my hand. It'll be OK," he nudges.

The terror rising, I realize this is a very real spiritual battle. "No!" I almost scream, "I need to get through this with the Lord!" Wow, what a super mature, religious thing to say! Then my husband does something totally out of character for him (note my judgment in that statement). He steps up. Normally he would throw up his hands and walk away exasperated with my tough self-reliance and "let" me have it "my" way. Not today. He does *not* listen to me. My strong, handsome husband comes to me (note my change of attitude). He puts his hand out and says in a powerful, sexy tone, "You do whatever you need to do with God [he honored my need to wrestle through this spiritually], but I *want* you take my hand. We are going to do this *together*." I took his hand, prayed in every kind of tongue my mouth would pray, and pressed to the edge. I stood there, palms running with sweat, looking over that beauty—way down there—and got over it.

The King gave me utterance to battle the enemy and my husband gave me his hand to hold on to. Halfway off of the lookout, walking in peace and confidence, I start to thank the Lord out loud for giving me victory. Suddenly I get a little movie in my head. The Holy Spirit shows me my husband reaching out his hand to me. Then He says, "Jamie, I *want* you take your husband's hand *and* mine. I gave him to you."

Oh, sweet sister, why won't you let him take your hand? Has he been untrustworthy? God is trustworthy. Has he been insensitive? God can reveal things to him if you will release them unto Him. Has he been unavailable? God will show you how to speak that to him. Whatever it is, sister, there is an answer for you. Go to the Savior, seek Him, and ask Him about *you*. Ask Him to change you—until you are changed.

Chapter 5

LEFTOVERS

W E ALL HAVE leftovers in our lives. And, no, I am not talking about that blue container in the way back left of your refrigerator that looks like it very well might be penicillin. I encourage you to take it out, open it, and get rid of it, even if it's going to gag you for a minute. It will be well worth it in the end. We all have incidents in our pasts that are very much like that blue container. We believe they have had absolutely no impact in our lives, and we have even forgotten some of them for a very long time. Then, without warning, there they are, right out in the open for all to see. The unfortunate thing is that leftovers are usually seen much sooner by others than by us.

Devaluation

Let me tell you the "bacon story" from one of the very early years of our marriage and shortly after I had come to Christ. My precious husband, being great at finding a good deal, frequently buys our biweekly groceries. This particular day I had a written list of low or no inventory items. On that list was not the normal *one* but instead *two* packages of bacon. I didn't want to argue about the quantity, so I just didn't mention it to Jim. I just hoped he would pass it by as a request to fulfill a certain recipe. We had not gone over the list before he left, so it was just recorded there for him to follow. (It wasn't until years later we figured out it was a great idea to go over the list verbally before he went on his shopping excursions. That would be communication, people.)

Anyway, upon his arrival home from shopping, Jim comes up the stairs hauling bag after bag of his precious deals. I begin to empty the parcels in anticipation of my two packages of bacon. No bacon, no bacon. Aha, a bacon! Another bacon? Check the bag again; just *one* bacon. "Jim?" I called. "Yeah," replies my shopping hero. "Did you 'forget' the other bacon?" I inquired, not wanting to imply a malicious act. "No, I didn't think we needed two bacons and they were pretty expensive," he innocently responded.

Well, the floodgates *blew* open! A dam of emotions took to the brink! I *ran* to my room and closed the door; yes, I "closed" it, I'm not a slammer. I *bawled* and *bawled* until I could bawl no more. My husband entered the room, wondering why I had abandoned my job of putting the groceries away, cold stuff and all. He stood in the doorway astonished at the sight before him. There I am, on the floor, eyes swollen from crying, Kleenex piled around me. "Leave me alone," I sobbed. He honored my request and backed slowly out.

In an earlier day I would have made him sit by me and try to "pry" the truth out. Ultimately I wouldn't have shared the truth anyway. I might have said, "Nothing, I'm *fine!*" He would have left thinking he was bad and with no clue why. His "leftovers" told him he was bad and he accepted it. I would have come up with some very clear reason in my mind as to why he was a jerk, felt some self-justification in it, and got on with my day, leaving us both wounded and with zero resolved. But enough of that, we will talk that syndrome over in the "Is It Medical?" chapter.

My new walk with the Lord had begun to change me. This day was different. I knew I needed let the Lord help me to begin to see *me*. I sat on my bedroom floor and I sought Him: "Why did I react like this, Lord?" Hadn't I always been able to let things just roll off of my back? The reality was that before Christ my wall of defense was big and thick enough to convince me that I just didn't care.

I was also just too tough to bother dealing with past issues. In fact, I thought I was so tough that I didn't have past issues! Now, lying on my bedroom floor, I was finally open to let my King over that wall. OK, maybe let Him take one brick down and allow myself to look inside at *me* for once—not at my husband, not at my desires; just at my behavior and me. "God, I want to be different." With my eyes closed, the Lord began to show me a picture.

I was about fourteen and my family was seated around the table for the big breakfast Dad always made on Sundays. I loved this time. Our whole family was there, and it reminded me of the Cleavers somehow. We passed around the heaping plate of hot French toast and the scrambled eggs, and then Dad would hand out two slices of bacon to each of us. As the food would pass by, I would strategically place each item in its spot and prepare for the dig in. The bacon was my favorite so I *loved* to save it for last. "Pass the French toast again, please." Ah, time for my bacon; *my* bacon! Only *one* piece of bacon? I *had* two! We all get two! I looked around to see if I had "dropped" my other piece. I look up and my dad is smiling. He had reached over when I wasn't looking and took one of my bacons!

The tape in my teen mind starts to roll to *another* place where he takes from us kids and does for him. I can't tell you if this happened once, twice, or several times over the years; but I can tell you, along with other strong messages, it left a mark deep in my persona. Somewhere in my heart I received the idea that men will take whatever they can, men only think about themselves, men cannot be trusted, and my desires are of little value. Daddies should always look out for their kids first, right? My Jesus walked me through the little movie revealing all of the *false* beliefs I had believed and received.

Oh, my goodness! "I didn't lose it over bacon, Lord; I lost it over *value*! I *am* valuable, Lord! I *am* loved and cared for by You, Lord! I forgive my dad (he thought it was funny) for taking my bacon! This has *nothing* to do with my husband or bacon, Lord." Wow! I am messed up. I need to go explain this to my husband.

When I walk into the kitchen, my shopping hero was finishing my job. So many times before I would have held him at arm's length with criticism or silence (after all he should be able to "read my mind" and *know* why I was hurt); but not this day. I will allow myself to be vulnerable. "This is what healthy people do, Lord. They communicate." "Jim, I need to tell you why the bacon was such a huge thing for me . . ." As I shared, I took that stinky blue container out, opened it, gagged on it, and threw it out of my life. My husband listened. And with tears in his eyes, he said, "Jamie, I'm *not* your dad." I asked for forgiveness and took out the trash, done with that old container of leftovers.

Today we laugh about the "bacon story." Do you know what your bacon story is? Do you wonder why you react in a terribly inappropriate way to circumstances at times? You are not crazy, nor are you demanding and cruel; you want your bacon! Do you desire to offer a three course meal in your marriage and are finding there are only leftovers available? What have you brought into your marriage that is your parents', your siblings', your old boyfriend's, a scar from an incident at school? What has been spoken over you, into you, or around you that you still believe? I found out that having two packages of bacon was not the way to heal those thoughts. Yes, I do have as many pieces as I choose now, but I know that does not heal past hurts.

Will you ask King Jesus to look in your refrigerator with you and take those containers and rid yourself and your marriage of the rot? It has been thirty years since my bacon incident, and I will tell you there have been many more. I still get before the Lord and ask Him to continue to show me what leftovers I am "in" from my past. Only being open, honest, and willing to look inside of you will heal these things. Jesus waits for you to allow Him to go there with you.

REJECTION

One of the areas that is so prevalent with many women is rejection by their fathers. Whether it is divorce or abandonment or chemical, sexual, verbal, religious, or physical abuse or whatever other unnamed thing that has damaged you, know there is hope. Many women are going through their relationships with a horribly damaged heart. Some of them are acutely aware of their condition and some of them are totally unaware until they crash or are confronted by it. Is that you today? Will you go to the Lord and ask Him to show you anything that has caused you to bring leftovers into your relationship with your husband?

Maybe looking at a few of these questions will help. Are you constantly looking to men for affirmation? Are you a "people pleaser," especially with men? Are you promiscuous? Do you have fears or insecurities in your marriage that make no sense? Do you allow things with men to happen to you that you should not? Are you defensive with your husband? Do you have an eating disorder, chemical issue, or behavioral issue? Are you super passive? Needless to say, overt anger toward men in general is a pretty strong clue.

I got a "clue" one day. I had spent years of my adult life trying to please my dad. When I was around him I was super "in tune" to where he was, what he was doing, and how I could "help" him or say something that would impress him. This particular day my four-year-old daughter came running out of the bathroom, her bottom naked. She had just gone potty and was having underpants issues. From behind his newspaper in the other room, my dad yells, "Look there, she is just like her mom! She can't keep her pants on either!" Standing in the kitchen, out of his view, my heart broke, tears welling up.

His reference to my teenage pregnancies was devastating. I had made poor choices in my teens (looking for love from a man). Even though I was now married and raising three precious little girls, Dad taunted me about my past. It was another disapproval from the one from whom I so desperately wanted approval. I went home that day with a broken, heavy heart, so ashamed of my past and myself. The hope that I ever had that I would please my daddy was lost.

The next morning, with the whole family out of the house, I faced it head-on. The pain that I had suffered the day before had now festered into a rage that I almost couldn't contain. Even though I was new to the Lord, I *knew* I had to bring all of this pain and anger to the altar. I was sick of being shamed, disapproved of, and rejected by men. I got in the shower—a place of vulnerability. I played the scenario of the previous day over and over in my head. Then I saw many other scenarios where my dad had been abusive, detached, and disapproving. The rage building, I began to shake my fist and yell, "Where were You, God? Where were You when he was...?" I began to list all of the abuses and injustices. Crying so hard I began to wretch, I demanded of my King.

Then I saw Him. I saw my precious Savior right there; weeping—weeping at the choices of man, weeping at the innocent betrayed. He knew! He knows. Our King *knows* what it feels like to be wounded and treated unfairly; yet, He forgives. I knew I had to forgive my dad.

With the realization setting in that my Jesus was right there with me all of the time, I broke. Like streams of living water, I broke. The tears came and came and came. Falling on my knees in the shower in gut-wrenching pain, I mourned, "Daddy, why didn't you love me? Daddy, why did you beat me? Daddy, why do you hate me?" I cried. Hearing my own voice crying out to Daddy, I stopped. Why would I cry out to *him*? Am I crazy to *still* be crying out to *him*? I slumped to the bottom of the shower, running nearly cold now. Empty now, I lay there; broken. Then I felt Him. I felt Him in my heart, spirit, soul, and mind. It was my *Daddy*. He was enveloping me. I embraced Him. Then He spoke, "Jamie, if God is *for you, who* can be against you?" (Rom. 8:31). I felt it, heard it over and over in my head, and received it! Hallelujah! I rose to my knees and praised Him. I praised Him and I laughed, rejoiced, and laughed. If my earthly dad did not approve of me, it did not matter! If the King of the universe thinks I am awesome, then it is my dad's loss if he is not able to embrace me! Done! Done! Done!

Whom the Son sets free is free indeed (John 8:36)! I was set free that day, ladies. Set free from the *need* to have my dad's approval. How about you, precious daughter of the Most High, were you rejected by your daddy? Did your parents divorce and he was seldom "there" for you? Was he detached or absent? Did he hurt you emotionally, physically, sexually?

Maybe it was your mother who wounded you. I don't know. If you have deep, old wounds, you can be set free too! You must be willing to "look" at your leftovers, acknowledge them, and be willing to deal with them. Christ has freedom for you, if you are sick of being sick.

The next time I saw my dad was the beginning of a new thing. You see, when God touches the broken, He then restores it. I decided that I was going to love on my dad no matter if I got it back or not. So I did. This was a million years ago, but I remember it like it was yesterday. I walked into his kitchen. The newspaper was spread out on the table, and he was leaned over it, back towards me.

Deciding I was going to hug him (I had never hugged him as an adult), I counted to three: "One, I'm scared, Lord. Two, I am embarrassed, Lord. Three, here goes!" I leaned over and wrapped my arms around his neck; and not only did I hug him, I said, "I love you, Dad." Whoopee!

Now I wish I had a big "after story" to tell you; but I think I went into shock and I don't remember how he responded. I do know that it was the beginning of a whole new relationship for him and me. When my daddy, suffering from severe depression, took his own life many years later, he and I had a deep, intimate, godly relationship. Praise to the God of restoration!

Maybe your leftovers have formed a "pattern" in your marriage? My pattern follows several pathways, like these:

- See the problem
- Pray
- Try to fix it on my own
- Confront it
- Pray
- Watch it fall apart
- Be mad at God
- Shut down with my husband
- Rebel
- Finally get miserable enough to give it to the Lord and follow His ways

What is your pattern? Do you know your children are watching and learning your pattern? Do you keep your house beautiful and in order to please your husband; and then when he doesn't respond, do you wallow behind a book or a movie or maybe a shopping spree? Does your pattern include using *every* conversation to "work" on your relationship or his flaws, and then you can't understand why he would rather be with his buddies or in front of the TV or video game? Do you just not say anything at all and keep your little self all safe in that blankie of self-pity?

Remember how I said earlier that I still get before the Lord and ask Him to show me things from my past that bring "leftovers" into my marriage? Well, I do. It has been from issue to issue that my Savior has freed me up and healed me. Let me share a more recent phase. I need to call it a phase because I have found that all of the areas in which the Lord has set me free come in phases. I believe He does this because our flesh can only handle so much ripping; then we can receive and go on to the next ripping. I say "ripping" in the most precious sense of the word.

INFIDELITY

For twenty-one years of my marriage, my husband worked locally. He was home every day for lunch, called several times a day, and was home doing his projects on his days off. After many years of discontent at his longtime employment, the Lord, through circumstances, freed him from that job. We moved to allow my husband to go to college, and then we moved again to relocate for his new job. We had always lived very near all of our family, so the move that took us four states away was a huge adjustment for both of us. Being married as teens we were very young empty nesters, so we viewed this as our "adventure" without any kids for the first time in our marriage.

Jim's new job required a lot of travel. We had chosen this profession for that exact reason. We wanted to see the world and experience things for the first time "kidless." I purposely did not take a job, as we wanted me to be free to travel with him. We were well aware of the ungodly behavior of many men that travel, and we were bound and determined to protect our marriage and have a great time together with this new opportunity. Jim started his career with a few short trips. I chose not to go as I was trying to establish some friendships and a relationship with a church body. Things were going smoothly and our transition was bringing us closer. Then it happened. He came home from the office one day and informs me that he is being sent to Taiwan—for six weeks. Because of the remote location and accommodations, I can't go. My heart jumped; then it fluttered; then it pounded!

My head began to plan things I could join or visits I could make to help pass the time. I was going to be alone in a new area for a very long time. My head was telling me I was going to be fine. In fact, because we'd been married since I was seventeen, I was kind of intrigued about learning "who" I was without my husband around. But my heart kept pounding. With a stiff upper lip, I sent him packing.

The first few days went by. I managed well for a girl who was used to her husband coming home for lunch every day. On about the fourth day, my husband calls me and reports the conditions where he is staying, what his days consist of, and what the country is like. Then, bless his heart, he starts to share. He tells me how the "guys" go out at night and get prostitutes, go to nude bars, and have women sleeping in their rooms—the single guys *and* the married guys! There it is again—pound, pound, pound. My heart is pounding out of my chest! That night I lay in bed with visions of tiny little women offering themselves to my husband on the street—pound, pound, pound. I slept…a little. The next day I called my husband in Taiwan three times. That night I lay in bed knowing that the tiny little women had, in fact (he told me), grabbed my husband's arm and begged him to come with them—pound, pound, pound; tears. I slept…a little. The next day I called my husband in Taiwan *six* times. Really, I did.

This went on for about three weeks, every night with the pounding, crying, and little sleep happening. Then one night I snapped. The enemy came like a flood and attacked. You see, if he can get you sleep deprived, you are vulnerable. He loves to prey on the weakened. I pictured my husband with a prostitute and heard the words from the enemy, "Do you really think calling him six times a day will keep him from being unfaithful? Aha! He didn't answer when you called." Where was he? Pound, pound, wail. "My God, *help me!*" Satan had brought every vile picture and every false accusation and fear imaginable to my mind.

Just when I thought I would snap, God answered, "Jamie! Do you think I have brought you *this* far to have your marriage fail?" It was His voice; His presence; His reassurance. "No, Lord, of course You didn't." There was a holy hush in the room. I received His words, took control over my emotions, in great fury rebuked the enemy, and stopped calling my husband in Taiwan six times a day.

I slept well the rest of the night, but I got up in the morning knowing I had to deal with this issue. I was flabbergasted at what was going on with me. Where did this come from? My husband has *always* been faithful and very integrous with his eyes. Why is it showing up now? I need help!

I went to my small group for church that evening. After the teaching was over, we always had personal ministry time. When the pastor's wife asked if anyone needed prayer, she looked right at me. I was brand-new to this body, overwrought with confusion, and did not even know them well enough to know if I could trust them with something this weighty. But, I was desperate. I stood up, walked to the "prayer chair," and said, "I need prayer." I shared with them what I had been going through. The pastor's wife said I had probably always had this insecurity but it had never been "tested" because my husband and I had never been apart. That made sense; except for, "Great, this has been here all along?" I am very outgoing and confident, I have no body issues, and I love my life. Can this be for real? So they pray.

Oh, my sister, if you have been resistant to the ministry of personal prayer, please stop. Stop right now and ask the Lord to bring down your wall of pride, mistrust, or whatever, and to enable you to humble yourself and go for prayer. Let others lift you and gird you up. It is a God thing.

So they pray and I weep. I have been so blessed in my life to have people mature enough in the Lord to be able to pray and listen to the Lord and know when *not* to speak. These precious saints press in for me and they are silent. As I weep, the Lord shows me a picture. It was a man with a woman, and then another woman, and then another. Pound, pound, pound. "Oh, Lord, please don't make me see my husband having sex with another woman!" The Holy Spirit says, "Look closer, Jamie." As I search my mind's eye, I focus in. There he is; it is my very own daddy with other women. You see, in his years of alcoholism, my dad had many affairs; affairs with women who would drink with him while Momma was home taking care of her family.

Have you ever had revelation, sisters; huge revelation? Well, I did; right there and then. As I looked at Dad's behavior, I *saw* what a horrible example he was to this little girl. He put into my spirit that all men have affairs. It was *not* my husband, who has been faithful to the nth degree! It was my very own dad. There is always a lie, sister; always a lie the enemy puts into our minds. We can receive it and make love to that thing, or we can rebuke it.

I began to forgive my dad, out loud, for being a horrible example in that area. I forgave him right there, speaking out forgiveness as I bawled in front of strangers. When you are sick of being sick, you will not care who sees your pain. When I was done praying, the pastor's wife lovingly looks me in the eye and says, "I knew it was your dad, but I knew *you* had to 'get there.'" Again, praise God for the mature in Christ who listen and allow Him to do the work. I got freed up right then and there from the bondage. I am talking bondage! I went home that night laughing. When my husband called me the next day, he was worried something was wrong because it had been twenty-four hours since we had talked. I was so set free that I didn't *need* to call him incessantly.

I slept. I prayed for my husband to be strong if tempted. I began to *let go*. I will be honest with you; even though the bondage was broken that night, I had to "walk out" the freedom. Every time the enemy tried (and still tries occasionally) to come back at me with a thought or fear of infidelity, I stood against it. I released my husband unto the Lord. I continued to dig into that old container and toss out the leftovers.

DISHONOR

Before we finish this chapter, I have to address something that I feel really grieves the Lord. I see it in Christian and secular woman. The enemy has, through whatever sick means, turned a large number of women into true *man haters*. I am not talking just the gal who is fresh out of a nasty divorce and is still seething with revenge, betrayal, woundedness, or whatever. I am including general jovial putting down of men all the way down to deep disdain for them.

I will remind you; if you are a Christian woman and you even a little bit dislike men in general, you are in sin. God has ordained from the beginning that they are *over* us in order (1 Cor. 11:3). I did *not* say lording it over us. I said over us in *order*. First of all, we are commanded to love one another—man or woman (John 13:34). Second, men are in authority, not because they are better but because of order. We do not have a problem with obeying our boss, male or female, because they are our bosses. We understand the "order."

So I am going through life hating men. My story goes like this: I am a product of an affair where a man is unfaithful to his wife with her little sister—scumbag. Then I am adopted into a home where Dad is an alcoholic, unfaithful, and physically abusive—creep. Then boys use me for sex when I just want them to love me—perverts. Then I marry a man with anger and detachment issues—jerk. How's that for you? If that's not "leftovers," I don't know what is! Do you have a sadder story than I do? Very possibly you do. I am in *no* way making light of your pain. I am, however, trying to help you to see the possible bitterness, unforgiveness, and mercilessness in yourself that may be damaging your own current marriage.

Have you ever looked at how those vile emotions look on someone else? Watch the venom spewing from a scorned woman's mouth. It's very unattractive and unappealing. How about the dull look on the depressed woman's face from years of suppression, her harbored pain eating away at her joy? We are out there. We are out there with many different masks on. How do you feel about men today? Really, how do you feel?

My dishonor and disdain of men was an area that had what I would call a generational hold on me. Besides the aforementioned rejections from men in my life, I possessed a very deep-seated, long-held hostility towards men. Let me tell you how that carried out in my life. This may not line up with some peoples' theology, but this is how it has played out in my life.

Through my years of walking with the Lord, He revealed to me many areas where I had "interjected" a disdain for men. One of those was with my desperate desire to have a son. When I had just turned sixteen, I aborted a little boy at sixteen weeks gestation. That story is written in another book, *Passion Child*. Then I marry a man that is the very last male to carry his family name. I go on to have three daughters. I so wanted to have a little boy for my own healing and to carry on my husband's name. After not producing a son naturally and several unsuccessful attempts at adoption, we realized we would not have a son.

I went to my Word one day, inquiring of the Lord why He would not allow me to have a son.

He lead me to the Book of Hosea that read, in part, "Because...your hostility is so great...Ephriam's glory will fly away like a bird—no birth, no pregnancy, no conception" (9:7, 11). I dropped to the floor and wept. My hostility toward men would keep me from having a son? "God, forgive me!"

I began a very long journey of repenting, rebuking, and healing in that area of my life. God also gave me some very godly men to allow me to "see" their awesome uniqueness, covering, and calling in life. I knew my restoration was complete when a series of awful and wonderful events took place.

My back started to hurt. I *never* have a backache; we must need a new mattress. Three months later back still hurts. It is not the mattress; my back still hurt visiting my mom this weekend and her mattress is brand-new. After six months (I know, I'm stubborn) I go to see the doc. He comes back with the full report. I have gallstones. He advises that I have surgery immediately. Well, I hate to inform him but I have a *very* busy several weeks coming up. I am going to Oregon for three weeks to visit my brother and then to Delaware for three weeks to visit my daughter. With the promise of eating all low fat and non greasy foods and my husband's hawk eyes on me, we leave on our trip. Surgery is scheduled the day after we return home.

Our trip to Oregon was fabulous, with the exception I had to eat like a bird. Then off to Delaware we went. Again we had a fabulous time, even though I still had to eat like a bird. While we were there, I attended a" tent church" in the middle of a corn- field. After praise and worship the pastor began his sermon. In the middle of it he stopped. He scanned over the congregation and made eye con- tact with me. I was certain I had stumbled upon a "children of the corn" cult and they were going to abduct me, never to be seen again. He says, "Lady in the white top [me], the Lord says to you: 'There is a new thing coming in your life.' Whatever that is will bring you great freedom and joy. It is almost like something is going to be removed and where it was will be replaced with bubbles, like a cleansing of sorts. I really do see bubbles and I feel that is sig- nificant to you." Little did he know that I *love* bub- bles! Someone after service brings me a tape of the "word." I leave, ecstatic about whatever it is that is to come. With our vacation over, we head back home.

Surgery went well. I got my picture of the pretty little stones that had been making my life miser- able and went home to recuperate. A knock on the door interrupted my nap. I called out to the person to come in so I wouldn't have to get up from my nest on the couch. It was Bev, a woman from a prayer group in our town but not from my home church. I had seen her before but really didn't know her. She greeted me and then began, "Jamie, I know you don't know me. And, honestly, I never do this. But this was so strong; I knew I had to obey. All I know is that this surgery you had is symbolic of a prophetic removal. Something has been spiritually removed from you, and it will never return." Wow! I knew this word was true as it "spoke" to my spirit immediately. So I sought the Lord.

I cried out, "Lord! What are you saying through this surgery?" It had now been years since the "emasculate" episode with Michelle. I had opened up and allowed many godly people to speak into my life on this issue. I especially let the Lord work on my heart attitude toward men, so I had experienced much healing. Don't get me wrong. I was *not* an outward, overt man hater. In fact, until I shared with people, they normally weren't even aware that I had an issue. Mine was an undercurrent of mistrust, angst, and viewing them as "perpetrators." As I prayed, the Lord showed me a little "rewind." I saw the Hosea scripture of my hostility towards men and how that robbed me of a son. I had, long ago, repented and was forgiven for that. Then I saw many other areas where I had repentance and cleansing of attitudes towards men.

All of a sudden I was in the cornfield church. Pastor's words rang loud and clear, "Something is going to be removed...like a cleansing of sorts. I...see bubbles." "Oh yes, Lord! You *said* I was going to have a 'removal' and a 'cleansing'! You also said, through Bev, that this surgery was a 'spiritual removal *never* to return'!" A scripture rushed to my mind: Proverbs 5:4: "In the end she is bitter as gall." Full revelation set in: The gall bladder produces bile. Bile is acidic and corrosive. "Lord Jesus, I have been bitter and acidic towards men, but you have been healing and changing that in me. It is done, removed, never to return!" Praise the Lord!

Now, sweet thing, do not for one minute think that I haven't had moments that I don't understand men or have a critical thought. But do understand that the generational, demonic hold in my spirit towards men was a finished deal that day. The years of repenting, opening up, pressing in, and letting go *precipitated* the awesome removal my King gave me that day. Just like the corn church, non-abductor pastor said, what *joy* and *freedom* to know that "thing" is forever gone!

So open up those doors, girls. We *all* have something in the refrigerator of our hearts. Go ahead, open the door, peer in, and let the Lord show you *your* leftovers. Open those stinky containers and start scoopin'. The King of glory will enable you to do whatever hard work is needed to get that fridge baking soda fresh!

Chapter 6

Get Off My Walk!

ODAY I'M GOING to meet with Kari. She
has asked me to be her mentor. I think this is very
funny. God will use the areas where you have struggled in your own life to minister to others, *if* you let
Him. Funny also because some of these areas I am
still struggling in. I ask Him if I should enter into
this position. He says yes.

The coffee shop is "brimming" with people (pun
intended). There really isn't a "quiet" corner to visit
in, so we sit smack in the middle of the establish-
ment in broad daylight with no cover. I am unaware
the level of emotion that is about to surface in my
new little mentoree. You see, when you allow things

to go for so long and do not reach out for help, you get to an emotional level that is way out of proportion. (Note to self: next time I have a first visit with someone, it must be in a more private setting.)

Kari barely has her little self settled in her chair when she bursts, and I mean *bursts* out, "I *cannot* stand it anymore, Jamie! I tell him and tell him and tell him! I show him what the Word says. I write posties all over the house so he can see the scripture every day. I subscribed the men's Christian magazine for him, signed him up for the men's prayer group, and called all of the men to "invite" him to all of the events at church. When, when, oh, *when* is he going to follow the Lord? I told him he must lead this family or God will deal with him! I explained to him that our children will go to hell and one of us will have an affair if he doesn't pray every day, read scripture over us, and attend godly things. God is a just and fair God and He will not be mocked—blah, blah, blah!"

So I'm doing one of these in my head, "Really, Lord? Really?" When I am done having my little tantrum in my head, I start to seek the Holy Spirit. "Father, show me how to respond; what would You have me say?" Kari finishes her tirade with, "What should I *do*?" "Ah, thank You, Lord." I love it when someone gives me a carte blanche opening. With me, don't ask if you don't *really* want to know.

"Stop it," I quietly respond. She does "stop" but not "it." She *stops* long enough to pause and processes what she "perceives" is my *inability* to understand what she has just described and then begins to reiterate every word she just said with much more passion and volume. I love that about people who don't want to listen; they repeat either verbatim or switch it up a bit, thinking we must not have "heard" them. I let her get about one quarter into the tirade again, and I lean across the table into her space. "Stop it," I interrupt. Frustrated now, she throws up her hands and squeals, "What do you mean 'stop it'?" I wait to see if she is done and *really* ready to "hear." I reach across the table now to touch her wrist. She needs to know that I am "for" *her*, but *not* against her husband. I am "for" *them*. She needs to know I mean what I mean.

"Kari, how long have you been doing this?" I ask tenderly so as to expose the absurdity in it yet empathizing. She begins to go "into it" again. "Stop, stop, stop!" I plead. I pause and ask again, "How long?" Incredulous, she squeals, "Nine years! I have been doing this for nine years!" I let that hang there for a minute. We are now the focus of said coffee shop. She looks around and then back to me. I really want to use the Dr. Phil "how's that working for you" statement, but I suppress the urge. "Kari, Moses is dead," I state. She is quiet now. I am sure she is sure that I am crazy referring to Moses' death and all. If nothing else, it stops the tirade. I carefully inquire, "Where is the scripture that says *you* have to bring your husband to Jesus? Doesn't the Word say that Jesus will draw man unto Him?" (John 12:32). She is about to go into the wild thing again when I firmly ask, "Do you or do you *not* want this to change?" "I do," she surrenders. Beginning to understand that she, unlike Moses, has *not* been called to bring her husband to the Promised Land, she acquiesces and we dig in.

You see, ladies, we are *not* called to teach *or* preach to our husbands. Now this is not the "don't be over a man" teaching (1 Tim. 2:12). I have led Bible studies with men in them, including my husband. He, however, was there of his own free will, knowing that I was the teacher. This is the "this does not work, ladies; been there done that, do not try this at home" lesson. I am so not kidding about this. We have to ask ourselves *why* we feel we are responsible to "lead" him to Jesus. Do you do that to your boss, coworkers, or neighbors? No, we "minister" to them so they see the precious path of grace and *desire* to walk it. Yet we beat our husbands over the head with scripture, lessons, Christian television, conferences, praise and worship music, and on and on.

Get off his walk, sister! Honestly, many times this is fueled by selfish pride. So often we want our husbands to "know" Jesus with our main motive being our own comfort. We go into what I call "Christian gaga mode." This is when you fantasize about his walk being so strong that he prays over everything from sex to finances. You are fulfilled and prosperous and your life is better in every way. You are missionaries or ministers and bring hundreds to

Christ as a way of daily living. Oh, and there is the one where he is going to be so sensitive in the Spirit that he will know every need you have. That was *my* personal favorite. See, I *know*; I've been there.

Oh, sweet sister, whatever your gaga fantasy is about, can you see the selfish pride in that? It is selfish because it is for your own gain and pride because it is all about *you* and *your* desires. Know that our hearts and prayers are to be for our husbands' salvation and their walks with Christ. They are a work in progress—not under *your* construction! So this chapter is about your husband's walk or lack thereof; *not* your business, except for prayer and encouragement. Let it go, honey. *His* walk is *his*; *your* walk is *yours*. I find that I have so much to work on in my own walk that I don't have time to work on his.

Many of us are married to unbelievers. My husband will tell you that his position with the Lord right now is that he is "on the fence." He has been there for over twenty years. I am sorry if that discourages you. Pray for my husband. Maybe by the time you read this he will be walking with the King. I do not know. I *do* know that I am ashamed to admit I have done so many things to beat him, drag him, shame him, plead him, and chase him to Jesus. I am not sure you could find a ploy I haven't already tried.

Now I need you to back up just one minute with me. My past had a deep impact on my *perception* of marriage and that affected me in my campaign for my husband's salvation. Coming from a home wrought with alcoholism, infidelity, and dysfunction, I had stepped into the child-parent-fixer position, always intervening in grown-up issues.

What does this have to do with my husband's on-the-fence position with the Lord and my position in that? It has everything to do with it. You see, my friend, *I* had to "fix" my husband's walk. Remember leftovers? I was just walking the position I was forced into in my home. After all, that is what my past told me to do; be the fixer. You must fix it; no one else will. You know how to do this; he *needs* you. Leftovers, pumpkin; it was leftovers. Did Jesus ask me to do this? No.

What are your leftovers in this area? Why do you feel you are your husband's Moses? Is it something from your past? Did you have a controlling mother? Do you really believe God will not bless you if your spouse is an unbeliever? Go to the Lord right now, my precious doll, and ask Him what is going on with you and your control of your husband's walk. Talk to Him about your fears. Why can't you let your husband's walk go? Why? It *is* all about you.

Sisters, I *ran* to Jesus when the Lord showed me my heart issue of trying to control my husband's walk. You see, one day I was whining to the Lord. Yes, I do this. "Lord, why, why, why aren't You talking to Jim?" I had been praying God would speak to Jim for so long. The Lord quips back at me,

"He isn't speaking to Me." Halted in my thinking, I saw the picture. It was my husband giving the Lord the silent treatment. Are you kidding? I saw Christ's form from the chest up, facing my husband. My husband was ignoring Him, going on with his daily busyness. Every time my husband moved, Christ would turn his body so He was ever "available" to my precious, oblivious man! I took in every detail of the picture. Then I had the most freeing revelation; Jesus Christ was *honoring* my husband's "no"! He was not stopping him, hanging on his leg, begging him. No, not our Jesus. He was by him; waiting, giving him choice.

It was then I received into my spirit the beauty of freedom in Christ, ladies. We have ultimate freedom to say no to the King of kings. Remember free choice? Yeah, it is for real! I remembered that day what the Lord had said to me years earlier, as I stood in wonder of Him and my salvation. He said to me, "Jamie, I have been calling you for ten years." Who am I to decide when another "should" come to Christ? I was so prideful that I would not honor my husband's decision to *not* heed. I repented. I *stopped*!

Next I had to look at my fears about him never walking with the Lord. Here it goes:

1. My children will become Satanists.

2. We will be divorced because a house divided cannot stand (Matt. 12:25).

3. We will not have the favor of the Lord on us, and his choices will hurt me and our kids; we will suffer.

4. I cannot minister to people if he is an unbeliever.

5. I can't go to church without him.

6. I was pregnant when I got married so I am being punished.

7. We won't have Christian friends.

8. I can't talk about and be a Christian without him.

9. I can't respect him if he isn't following Christ.

10. I want a godly husband!

I had yet to look at the core issue.

Will you look again at my list of fears? Will you look at *your* fears? I am asking you to lay this book down every time you *know* God is tugging at your heart. I need you to discipline yourself to do that. You need Him, not me.

Look at my list of fears again. Can you see my *core* issue? I see a couple things that are very apparent. The first one is the lies. The enemy had filled my head with so many lies; I was desperate for salvation for my husband out of fear. The second was the power I had given my husband. I really believed he held the power to ruin my life. Wow! Do you see it, though? Do you see my *core* issue? My core issue was that God was too small, not able to walk me through life with an unbelieving husband. Nope, my husband was bigger than God. Ouch! I was walking in unbelief and not trusting God with my life. Can you look at my list of fears and say out loud the "truths" in each area for me?

Are you full of fears and lies? If that is you today, you need to stop. How in the world do you have time to teach and preach at your husband when *your* walk is in danger? Stop with him and start with you. So let's start.

My friend from the coffee shop had a believing husband. He was raised in the church and knew the Word. He was just walking in disobedience; so was she. Now I could talk about him; but remember, this book is about her (us) not him. You see, besides usurping his authority and place in their home, my sweet friend was walking in a sin very familiar to me.

My little story goes like this. (I will have you know this is one of many similar stories; sometimes I am a hard learner.) Many times the Lord uses physical affliction to speak to me. If I am being stubborn, I might get a stiff neck. I had a sore throat for a week yet there was no redness in it; I could hardly speak. Yeah, I had been speaking pretty vile stuff to my husband. Anyway, on this particular occasion, the Lord showed me my sin very clearly.

We had purchased a fixer-upper home. For eight months we worked, doing much of the renovating ourselves including a bathroom I had just laid ceramic tiles two days earlier. A much-needed vacation was in order. I was preparing to go on a trip to Arizona to visit my mother the following morning on the 6 a.m. flight. Around 3 p.m. that afternoon, I began to feel a little irritation in my right eye. I used some eye flush, wet a cotton swab and swabbed at the lids, and forced tears to flush the "irritant" out. My eye was getting redder as I dug in it. I looked at the clock, which was approaching 4 p.m. "Lord," I prayed, "the eye doctor closes in one hour and I live thirty minutes out of town. I need this healed, Lord." I continued to ask the Lord to heal my eye—nothing.

I fully believe that this God of ours parted the Red Sea, and I knew He could heal my eye. I continued to ask until it dawned on me. "Lord, are You telling me something through this affliction?" And there it was, the little movie screen in my mind. I "saw" my husband wasting time in front of the TV, not fulfilling a desire I had laid before him and certainly not following the Lord. And then the still small voice says, "Why are you looking at the speck in his eye?"

"Oh no, Lord! I have had my eyes on *his* sin and been so angry and indignant about it. I repent, Lord! Please forgive me." I had been ignoring the Holy Spirit when He convicted me of judging my husband. I just kept stomping around. (In my heart, of course, because I am *way* too spiritual to behave like that outright.) At this point I cried for real. When I opened my eyes the horrible pain was still there. Then I cried some more. "Why, Lord? I repented. I have only forty minutes to get to town and the eye clinic will close. I called them and they said they would wait for me. Thank you, Jesus."

On the way into town, I inquire of the Lord, "Lord, why didn't You heal me after I repented?" He responded in a very fatherly tone, "Sometimes, after forgiveness, there are consequences to be paid." Of course! He had warned me again and again, and I would not listen. The doctor took one swipe and there it was; tile from my beautiful new bathroom— a tiny little shard, scratching with every blink. Ouch! I need to keep my eyes on Christ. Looking at others' failures and judging them hurts them, my Father, and me. My sister from the coffee shop had her eyes set on her husband not her Father.

Pride is an insidious thing. We wrap it in all kinds of false packages like "righteous anger," "speaking the truth," and "sharpening each other." All biblical, but not all walked out in the leading of the Holy Spirit.

I had a siren-blaring revelation not too long ago. My husband was in a different room and I overheard a conversation he was having with a little someone I hold very dear. The tone and delivery he used was very hurtful. I could not believe my ears. I went into a different room and "told Jesus on him." The whole rest of the day I planned what I was going to say to him when I confronted his behavior. My emotions were very high and I was *right* about his behavior not being acceptable. I ranted to the Lord, "I am *horrified* at what he did and said. How could he? I am going to..." I played out the confrontation in my head. As I "watched" this confrontation, I saw my husband before me. I was laying out the infraction before him when the Lord tersely interrupted, "Jamie! This is Jim's sin. It is no different than anyone else's sin (including yours). Are you going to argue him out of his sin?"

Duh! Of course my husband wasn't going to slap the heel of his hand on his forehead and exclaim, "Wow, honey! Thank you for chastising me in anger. You are right. This is sin! Thank you so much for pointing that out." This was an area that he had struggled in for years. I have no idea why I thought I was going to bring him to "fresh revelation" that day. I, however, had a big old Jesus lightbulb moment. Suddenly I had a new understanding. God's perspective on sin is not the same as mine. God saw my husband's sin and hated it. Yet, He sees my sin and hates it also. I have sin that is a stench to the Lord. So do you. So does your husband. In my pride, I perceived Jim's sin as horrific and my sin as a slight infraction. We sin against God. It is horrific!

So, I am in the coffee shop with Kari. "Stop teaching and preaching and let him go, Kari" I pleaded. "But I am married to him! How do I do that? Do I stop talking about God in my house? Do I stop praying?" she cried. "You do what the Holy Spirit tells you to do. Read the Word, surround yourself with women who love the Lord and you, and pray," I encouraged. I knew, for her, this would be a whole new way of living. She had a ton of leftovers running her engine. But God! God is bigger than you and will show you if you let Him.

When you have truly let go and gotten "off of his walk," you will know. You will not only stop teaching and preaching but your prayers will change. I remember before I understood this "letting go" my prayers would go something like this: "Lord! My husband is doing blah, blah, blah. I am asking You to convict him and show him his sin. Whatever it takes, Lord, You get him!" Yeah, one time when I was praying a "get 'em" prayer over someone, the Lord said to *me*, "Are *you* ready?"

I need to be open to anything God has for all of us—correction, rebuke, and chastisement. Yikes! If my heart is loving and pure, I will pray those things I desire for me also. So you might begin to see some evidence in your prayer life *for* him not against him. Do you really think the Lord is looking to and fro wringing His hands in eager anticipation to "get" someone? Uh-uh, no! He is *for* us. I heap prayers of love on my husband's head now. "Oh, that he may know You, Lord. Bless his heart that he may feel Your presence. Loosen the chains that keep my precious husband bound. Lead him and protect him. Heal him, O Lord. Help me to release him. What would You have me pray, Lord?"

So as you let his walk go, you give him the freedom to grow and seek Christ or not. First Corinthians 7:17 says, "Nevertheless, each one should *retain the place* in life that the *Lord assigned* him to and to which God has called him" (emphasis added). Are you ready to walk *your* walk? Are you walking *your* walk? So many women have told me that they did not go to church or raise their children in church because their husband did not want to go. Sisters, when you stand before the Lord and He inquires of you why you did not follow Him, is your answer going to be, "But Bob didn't want to, Lord"? The Lord will reply, "Who is Bob?" It won't wash ladies, it just won't wash. You are responsible for *you*. He is responsible for himself. We stand before the Lord alone, not married.

I am ashamed to say that my husband walks out some godly principles way better than I do. I remember going through several very hard "breakings" in the spirit. My husband would perceive my pain or see my swollen eyes from crying and gently ask, "You OK?" "No, I am not. God is doing a work in me and it really hurts." "Wow, I'm sorry, can I do anything?" he would ask. I would say no and he would say OK and walk away without asking for one detail. He gave me the freedom to walk my walk.

Kari is letting go and walking her walk. The Lord has been heaping love on her Spirit. Her husband is miserable—poor man. God is doing a work in him—blessed man.

Chapter 7

GIVE YOUR WHOLE HEART

*S*O, WE ESTABLISHED in the intro that you are a follower of Christ. When I came to Christ, I was the crazy don't-answer-your-phone-'cause-she's-a-new-Christian girl. For real! I was so zealous I just *had* to cram Jesus down everyone's throats. Who cares if they choke a little? They *need* Jesus. Bless their hearts; the mature helped me to tone it down to a palatable measure. But, I have a really sad story to tell you.

I loved the Lord for seventeen years before I found out I had a huge idol in my life. I am not kidding! Now don't go turning to the next chapter because you don't think this applies to you. Trust me, this chapter *will* apply to you, I don't care who you are. You see we get so "spiritual" that we can't see our own junk. We also are lacking, at times, a true biblical understanding of what an idol even is. I get concerned that we don't hear much from the pulpit anymore about idols. We have a sense that they are statues from the Old Testament—not so.

Matthew 22:37 says, "Love the Lord your God with *all* your *heart* and with *all* your *soul* and with *all* your *mind*" (emphasis added). Period; end of discussion. Now let's be honest here. Without Christ, we *cannot* even fathom what that looks like. How do you give *all* of your heart, soul, and mind? I don't know. But He does! I, to this day, seek the Lord to enable me to love Him with all that I am.

HUSBAND IDOLATRY

So, back to my sad story. Did I tell you I had this revelation *after* seventeen years of walking with Him? Yeah, I did. I just needed to say it again because it seems so ridiculous to me. Anyway, so I felt led to attend a women's weekend just down the road from me. I had no idea why God would have me to go. The pastor's wife from my new church called, inviting me to join her. I told her, "Indeed, I will go." I hung up the phone and grinned. I was thinking, "O Lord, You are so cute. I get to get acquainted with her in our pj's."

I arrived at the conference and found that the main speaker was a woman from a large city several hours from us. I had previously had an "encounter" with her that was a little unpleasant. So my first "issue" was to get before the Lord and get my heart right towards her so I could receive fully what she was sharing that weekend. So, I did. With my heart right, I settled into the comfy seat next to Veronica, pleased we would have some bonding and growth in the Lord time together.

The speaker introduces herself and proceeds to reveal what God has put on her heart for a topic for the weekend—idolatry. Ugh! "Really, Lord?" I, like you, was *convinced* I had no idols in *my* life. Now, certain I was there only for fellowship with Veronica, I acquiesced to a perceived very "dull" weekend as far as teaching went. (I sure hope preconceived notions are not a sin.) At least I could now just focus fully on Veronica, since I really didn't "need" the teaching. (Did I tell you I wrestle with spiritual pride on occasion? If you are very religious, you might even need to stop reading this book because, FYI, it is being written by a *sinner.*)

The speaker begins. I am scanning the room. "Cute hair! I know her from Life Church." The speaker continues. "Yummy, whatever they are making for lunch smells awesome!" Speaker is still speaking. "Oops! I better at least 'look' at the speaker now and then, after all, I am sitting in the front and people will see I am not listening. How rude, Jamie!"

I turn my head at the very second she makes eye contact with me and says, "If you are sitting here thinking you really don't need this teaching, then this is probably exactly what you need to hear this weekend." Well, that got my attention, kind of. I turned my body toward her and "listened" (in that challenging kind of way, like "oh yeah, I will listen. Let's just *see* if this is for me. Oh, yes, I am 'open'; yes, I am—kind of.")

She continues, "The Word specifically teaches that anything that is more important in your heart, mind, and soul than Christ is idolatry" Yep, I get that. Then she pauses (talking to the Lord, I assume), looks *directly* at me, and says, "And that, ladies, includes your husbands." I am honestly not sure if the gasp I heard was a corporate gasp from many women or if my gasp was so loud it just sounded like the whole assembly. Can you imagine? This woman just pulled the rug out from under the old "your husband is over you, he is the head, he is the leader" teaching.

Stop! I am not saying those are wrong teachings. I *am* saying that I, for one, had taken those teachings and put them in wrong order. Back to the story: I had one of those moments where the Holy Spirit *yells* at me and shoves a javelin in my heart and through my back and out the other side. Do you ever have those; when you know that you know that you *know* God is speaking to *you*? Well, ladies, that is what I had. Even though I was wrestling with my old understandings, I knew I needed to hear what this woman was about to say.

I want you to know, she spoke freedom into me that day. She continued, "Christ wants your whole heart…the whole thing. He doesn't say, 'Love the Lord your God with part of your heart and give the other part to your husband,' does He?" No, He doesn't! That is all I needed to hear. I got it. I had given my *all* to my husband. No wonder my heart, soul, and mind were always wandering; they are for Christ, not man. I wanted it. I repented right then and there of not loving my Jesus with my whole heart, soul, and mind. I asked Him to enable me to do just that.

The funny thing is that I felt a little like I had just ditched my husband. You see, when we are asked to do something in the Spirit, it just feels funky in the flesh. So, I kind of broke up with my husband…in the sweetest sense of the word. In fact, I had a little dance with another Man—my Christ. As the praise and worship band began, I got up and I danced with my Savior. I closed my eyes and felt His hand at my waist, His face gazing at mine, and He spoke sweetly, "Jamie, you have been chasing the wrong husband." As I allowed this new truth to soak, in I had a little panic. "What now? What in the world do I do with Jim now since I have given my whole heart to you, Lord?" I half laughed half cried. I felt the grin of the Holy Spirit; He replied, "You just love *on* him." Wow! Wow! I get it! I remember the scripture: "Love is patient, love is kind" (1 Cor. 13:4). "I get it, Lord! *Love* is a verb when it is with people. It is an action. Love with You, Jesus, is a state of *being*. It is who we are, Jesus. We are one; Your Word says so" (Gal. 3:28).

I have never been the same. Even though breaking up was hard to do, I had to. You see, when we take people off of the throne and release them to Jesus, it gives us the freedom to just love 'em. I had to take my husband down off of the throne I had put him on. I put him on the throne...above my Jesus. So sad!

Can I give you a clue or two to help you to see if you "might" have your husband as an idol? Many of these issues are mine and some of them from other women. See if you are in here. If not, ask the Lord to show you *if* this is or is not an area of idolatry for you.

I used to wake up in the morning and the *first* thing on my mind was wondering if my husband was going to be in a good mood or not. I would scan the day in my mind and see if there was anything I could do to make his day better. (I realized years later that my motive was desperation to please him so he would give me affection and approval. This was opposed to getting my affection and approval from my King. Remember, my leftovers left me "needy" for a man to approve of me.) I made sure what I was doing was up to my husband's speci-fications. Constantly, throughout the day, I was thinking of my husband, where was he, what was he doing, did he need anything? Second Peter 2:19

says, "A man is slave to whatever has mastered him." There it is. My whole day was spent with my eyes focused on my husband—my master. "Forgive me, King." Are you grasping what idolatry of your husband might look like?

When a difficult issue came up, my first reaction was to take it to my husband. I had my eyes on him for help first, not my King. Do you know the Word says? "It is better to take refuge in the LORD than to trust man" (Ps. 118:8). Do you follow your husband, your church, your friends, or good teachings? Or, do you follow Christ?

Red flags

I was so confused by "master" teachings at one time in my life that I sought counseling on the matter. My husband was not walking with the Lord. Everything taught at church seemed to be for couples, couples that loved the Lord. I chose a very mature, godly couple to go to for counsel. The husband was a "degreed" counselor and his wife drew alongside him. I felt confident and safe with the two of them. My first visit went smoothly. The benefit of having a couple really ministered to me, as I knew we could cover male and female issues at one shot. The second meeting was much different. They began, "Jamie, you believe in Christ, right?" "Yep," I answered. They went on, "Do you believe the Word is true no matter what?" "Yep." "Well, then you believe that God has ordained your husband the head of your household, whether he is a believer or not?" "Yep." My red flags started to come a bit. "Well, then, you need to obey your husband in *all* things. If he is wrong then God will deal with him," they counseled. Big red flags!

Maybe they did not understand. I reiterated that my husband was not a believer. They said they understood that. I needed to be very clear what I was hearing. I asked, "Are you saying that if my husband asks me to *sin*, I should?" I am not kidding; they looked at each other, the husband grinning (he must have seen the shock on my face) and leaned in like he had a brand-new secret no one else was privy to, and said, "Yes." Then, leaning back like a wise old priest, he says, "You see, Jamie; it gets you totally off the hook. All of the responsibility is on your husband. Isn't that great?" They are looking in glee at each other now like they gave me this big nugget of "new truth" to live by.

Yikes! I so wanted to believe what they said. It was very attractive to think I would not be accountable for anything I was told to do by my husband for the rest of my life. But those red flags just kept waving and waving in front of me. I was more confused leaving that office than I had ever been in my walk. These were people I went to church with; they were elders and I highly I respected them.

I ran in the house and hit my knees. "Oh, my God; have I been walking in disobedience to Your Word? Do I not understand Your Word? I am so confused; help me!" I knew to grab my Bible. I begged the

Lord for clarity from His Word. God is so good. He brought me to stories in the Bible. One was the story of Ananias and Sapphira. Ananias purposefully withheld monies and lied about it. His wife knowingly followed him into the sin. They both paid with their lives. (See Acts 5:1–11.) This is why you must know the Word and why you must have a relationship with the Holy Spirit so you are not deceived. We are accountable for our own choices before the Lord, ladies. We will stand alone before the King one day.

I never went back to the "counselors." I went to my pastor and told him what I had experienced in the sessions. He confronted them, and they left the church. Again, please know the Word and have a conversational relationship with the Holy Spirit so you will *not* be deceived.

You would not believe the women I have met that do not attend church because their husbands won't and don't get spiritually fed because it makes their husbands uncomfortable. They engage in sexual practices that repulse them, detach themselves from loved ones, beg for money, allow abuse, stay silent, etc., because their husbands "said" so. We must come out of idolatry so, as couples, we can be free in Christ.

MARRIAGE IDOLATRY

This next area links closely so I won't say a lot about it. I would say this is a "Siamese twin" of husband idolatry. This is marriage adultery. For me, it took on a life of its own. I spent so many years fanning the flame of my marriage, I didn't even realize I was doing it. Writing this book has given me, again, such a clear picture of how that has looked in my life. Even now I have to laugh. Can you see me? I am around this fifteen-foot wide fire pit. In the very center of it is a teeny tiny little ember. I am running frantically around it with a cloth trying to "fan" the ember so it will "flame."

Every time I brought home another workbook on marriage, I was "fanning." Every time I signed us up for another marriage conference, another marriage Bible study, I was fanning. When I took hours on my knees pleading for a godly marriage, fanning. Oh, how about all that energy "assessing" your marriage, every day—fanning, fanning, fanning. Remember, my efforts in the "Can't or Won't" chapter? Dearest, it took me a bazillion years to figure out I was fanning a dead ember. Dead embers are a "won't." Honor the ember.

I was devastated as I pored through years of my journals for this book and found most of my prayers were about my marriage and not my walk with Christ. After I recovered, I was highly embarrassed. Seriously, if I would have run around and flapped my arms fanning any harder, I may have created a spark. What was I thinking? You see, the ember of my marriage was way inside the fire pit, unreachable because it was in the *wrong* place. It should have been at my Father's feet.

My focus on my marriage robbed me, sisters. It robbed me of a deep, intimate relationship with my Christ. I spent all of that time and energy fanning a *thing*, when I had life all along—life in Him. Have you given the throne to your marriage?

One morning over coffee I was sharing with my husband a very cool thing God had done for me. He responded with a "harrumph" (no words, just that), and then changed the subject. I was heartbroken. Later, on a walk with the Lord, I cried, "Father, this hurts so bad. Is it too much for me to want a response?" My Daddy responded (Do you see the lie of the enemy here? "I have 'no one' to talk to"; *lie*—I have Christ to talk to.), "Jamie, what if he *never* responds? Have I given you friends to share Me with? Does his lack of communication negate all that he is?" Wow! You see, *my* idea of a perfect relationship is one loaded with communication. Communication is how I *feel* loved...my love language. Is it my marriage's responsibility to fill that whole cup? Absolutely not! Grow up, Jamie.

Is that you? Do you suck the life out of your marriage? Are you needy? Do you expect your husband to chase you if you shut down? Do you always want him to be in a position of groveling for forgiveness? Does he have to fill your every desire? Do you resent he won't pray with you? Do you use the "D" word to keep him desperate for you? Are you sick or in pain all of the time so he has to baby you? Is he not the leader you want him to be? Does he not bring home enough money? Blah, blah, blah.

This is going to get disgustingly honest right now. I hope you can take it. I was seventeen and pregnant *on purpose* when I married. The motive for my marriage was to get me out of an abusive home and into a "good" family to be with someone who would be nice to me. Lies and deceit brought me to the marriage bed.

On my wedding night with tears were pouring down my cheeks and mouth agape in horror, I looked at the ceiling, groping for God, and screamed out in my heart, "My God! What am I doing?" I knew, ladies, I did not love this young man. I was not happy about spending the rest of my life with him and knew I fully intended on getting out as soon as trouble began. My motive for marrying him was *idolatry*—a savior from my dysfunctional home life. If you married because you were in love with the *idea* of being married, it's idolatry. If you married for financial security, it's idolatry. If you married because he was such a godly man, it's idolatry. Did you just want babies, a house, and a spouse? I don't know. I do know so many of us have married under idolatry.

Our true Knight in shining armor stood at the end of the aisle and waited for us; and we went a different way, chose a different husband. If that is you today, be honest, repent, and lay your marriage at His feet. If your idolatrous relationship is in horrible condition, good. Let the thing die, honey. When a seed dies and falls to the ground, it is then that the Lord can plant it, water it, and grow it how *He* meant it to be.

CONTROL IDOL

Maybe you have given your heart to control? Remember, we are talking about giving our whole heart to Him. If control is your God, then you just need to divorce her (Jezebel). Yep! I really do mean that. If you look at the demon of control as a for-real-gal, it is an ugly picture. If you are in charge; you are bossing; you are making the decisions; and you are running the house, car, money, kids, friends, church, clothes, and dog, get divorced from her. I am assuming you are still a Christian since you started this book. If so, why are you having an affair with this gal?

Are you confused why I am calling her a gal? Look closer, honey. If you are a control freak, then it is all about you. You have put yourself on that throne. Yuck! Obviously you have not taken your leftovers before the Lord and let them go yet. You might need to go back to that chapter; do a redo. You see, God is in control, darlin'. Get before Christ and repent of your need to control and repent of unbelief.

I am going to take a little rabbit trail on that one. Do you know if you make no decisions, make no waves, have no disagreements, you may still be a control freak? Yep, could be. You see, if you make sure the kids are quiet, the dishes are done, and the meal is ready; and you shop at the second-hand shop, don't speak up, hide your anger and disappointment, etc., out of fear and trepidation, then you are controlling. You think I am crazy, don't you? Can we look at it this way: you *don't* bring up his shortcomings because you don't want to "hurt his feelings or make him mad." OK, trying to protect someone from real emotions is *not* controlling? Ahem!

How about this one: don't make him mad? (This is one of my leftovers: don't make Dad mad.) When we "walk on eggshells," we are controlling. We are controlling the environment. Not only are we controlling our environment, but it is out of self-preservation. When we self-preserve we are telling the Lord we do not trust Him. So, we don't make him mad because we want to be comfortable. Ahem again. What if he did get mad? Will he self-destruct? Will he be uncomfortable? Will he die? Yeah, sounds ridiculous, doesn't it?

On the other hand, if you are truly *afraid* to allow him real feelings, you personally may have coping skill issues or you need to be honest about a possible abuse issue in your relationship. You see, when we allow ourselves and others to feel pain, we can work that through with Christ and grow. We see this patterned often in relationships where addiction is present. You might call in sick for him, hide his alcohol, make sure he doesn't get upset, and on and on. We won't let him fall. Falling is good, sisters; He is on the other side.

IDOLS OF EMOTIONS

Saddle up, ladies. The next idol we have in our lives is one of the biggest for women—emotions. Are you kidding? I minister to women almost daily. We have screaming, desperation, fatalism, tears, rage, vengeance, hysterics, doom, confusion, shut down, jealousy, and suspicion; need I go on? I have only one friend that has, to a great degree, overcome her emotions. Did you hear me? She *overcame* them! By that I mean she has dominion over her emotions, she is no longer *led* by them. Praise God! Even in times of great trial and attack, she can filter the information, process it, bring it to the Lord, and then respond in a mature, Christian manner.

I have to be honest; I have ridden this pony almost always in my marriage. I am able to have other relationships devoid of drama and heightened emotions. So for me, it might look like the story I told you previously. When my husband didn't respond to my story the way I wanted, I threw a big fat baby fit. I did. I began to do the very thing the Lord showed me I do. The part I didn't tell you was that on that walk, before I went to the Lord, I did one of these: "Boohoo! He *never* talks to me. We are done; there is no hope for this marriage." Then boohoo some more, "He doesn't even really love me. I bet this doesn't even bother him; boohoo." Really? So I have, now, through emotions, convinced myself that he *never* talks (lie; he is not mute), we are done (lie; we are still together), there is no hope for us (lie; with

Christ there is hope), he doesn't love me (lie and ridiculous; my husband adores me), and this doesn't bother him (lie; we talked it out when I got home). Whew! You see, I chose to negate all things about him, true or false.

What else? Oh, I know; this one is a good one I did with myself. "All men hate me." My birth father gave me away, my adoptive dad failed me, boys used me, and my husband is mean to me; so I have to keep trying to get them to like me. Yikes, huh? Well, the truth is that *He* will *never* leave me or forsake me (Heb. 13:5).

I call this kind of carrying on "making love" to it. What are *you* "making love" to? Are you just lying in bed with self-pity, arms wrapped around each other? Maybe you and rage have been making out on the couch? Oh yeah, he keeps whispering little ickys in your ear about your husband and you just kiss him back and tell him how right he is. You probably even have a bucket of ice cream in your lap, sharing it with him. Maybe you are just doing a little dance with fear. La, la, la—he is going to leave you. La, la, la—he is looking at other women. La, la, la—you are too fat for him to love you. Come on now, you *know* what I am talking about! Maybe you are used to a home that is always in chaos? If your leftover leaves you always wanting to pick a fight or you are just never content or grateful, maybe you are making love to chaos. Remember all the rotten things I said on my walk with the Lord? I was havin' a hoedown with a big fat deceiver—me! I didn't need the devil to chime in, I was doing fine just on my own. Our hearts, thoughts, and emotions *will* deceive us.

Yes, we also have an enemy that is alive and very active. Do you know that Satan magnifies negative things about our spouses in our minds? The thought will be there; we receive it, we begin to make love to it, and then it is full-blown meltdown. How would you feel if you knew your husband had bought into a lie of Satan about you? This doesn't happen very often for one simple reason: men do not usually allow their emotions to rule them. (Well, that's because they *have no* emotions, Jamie. No, no; bad girl!)

So many times our emotions take us near the brink. I almost gave up on my marriage once because I had totally bought the lie there was no hope for us. I was seeking the Lord about my hopelessness, and I saw a vivid picture. I was running on a racetrack and the finish line was getting closer and closer. I was straining under the effort, sweat running and muscles pumping. My knee was actually under the ribbon when the frame froze. I had stopped...just one pace before the finish line. I had total understanding. I was about to quit the race, just at the finish line. What if you quit? What if you give up on your marriage because you listened to your emotions? Then you get to heaven and God shows you the clip. You were one pace from victory in your relationship and you quit. Oh, sister, don't let it be. Don't let the enemy have a playground in your mind.

Our emotions are such a witness to where we are in our walk. When I hear Christian women use verbiage like

I was so afraid...

I cannot stand it...

I can't stop...

I hate...

I can't drive there...

I was so freaked out...

I was devastated...

I was crushed...

I'm afraid to be alone...

I need...

I thought I was gonna die...

I was shocked...

I won't...

Blah, blah, blah,

all that I hear is, "God isn't able; my emotions are more powerful than the King; the Word really isn't true; etc."

My little friend, Becca, called me one day. She was distraught. She shared with me that her husband had fallen asleep (gasp) while she was telling him something very dear to her heart. I was grinning to myself how cute she was in her very early stage of the "work" of marriage. "Jamie, I am just devastated," she wept. I waited for a moment and responded, "Becca, I bet that hurt, huh?"

I had been mentoring her for some time, so I felt at liberty to enter into the situation in depth with her. So I asked, "Becca, how old are you?" "Twenty five," she replied. "And how many years have you been married?" I continued. "Four," she answered. They had a precious two-year-old daughter, Hannah. I went on, "Becca, if you were told today that Hannah had leukemia, how would you *feel*?" "Oh, my gosh! I would be devastated!" she cried. "You would be devastated?" I prodded.

She was silent. "Do you hear what I am saying to you, Becca? I need you to look at the language that you are putting to your emotions." She was listening hard now. "Becca, you are *not* devastated that your husband fell asleep on you. Can we say you were hurt or disappointed? Would that be a more accurate word?" She giggled. "Yeah, I guess that was pretty dramatic; I guess I need to grow up, huh?" I answered her with, "I think it is time to put your big girl panties on, sister." We had a great laugh, and she went away with a whole new perspective.

Can I ask you the same today? Do you need to put your big girl panties on? Can I ask you to look at the words you use to describe your emotions? Are they true and valid for the situation? Or are your words dramatic and entertaining the enemy? When you tell your husband that you are "done" with him, are you really saying, "I am so hurt right now that I wish this pain would stop"? What is the *truth*? How can you find the truth? You can find it in a question: "Why am I so angry right now? Lord, why am I so angry right now?" He might tell you that you are not angry at all. He might tell you that you feel rejected. So instead of "I can't stand you." you will put big girl words to it and say the truth, "I feel really rejected right now and it hurts."

Sweet things, emotions are not bad. Emotions are from the Lord for good. They are a litmus test. If you have a heightened emotion, you need to ask yourself what is going on in *you*. "Why? Why am I feeling...?" When you express your heart to your husband with words instead of emotions, he will understand and draw near to you. When you express yourself with emotions, he will draw away. I am not, however, saying to stuff your emotions. We need to allow others to see our pain in the right motive and heart attitude. When we use them to manipulate, control, or lord over, we are in sin. You *can* have dominion over your emotions.

OTHER IDOLS

Ask God what you have on the throne in place of Him. Is it your past? Release your spouse from your past by looking at your leftovers, healing them up, and putting them at the Cross. Are you codependent? Oh yeah, if you are, you don't know you are, so it is redundant to ask that question. Let me help you; codependent people behave according to how someone else is behaving. If he is mad, you shut down. If he is frustrated, you try to fix it. If he is crabby, you have a bad day. I know; you still don't get it. If you have spent your whole marriage walking on eggshells—making sure he isn't mad, fixing all his boo boos, covering up his bad behavior, you are probably codependent.

He does not need you; He needs Jesus. Will you get *both* of you off of the throne and let go and let God do the work? Maybe you have put yourself on the throne for your husband. Does *he* walk on eggshells and try to keep you pleased all the time? Yikes! If that is you, *hurry*, get down from there. God wants His seat back.

Is your whole heart Jesus' or is your heart at Macy's? Don't laugh. I have someone very dear to me who chases shopping and not her King. Is your god *stuff*? Maybe it is food, drugs, alcohol, fear, anger, control, or people. It can even be something that is good. I have kept a prayer journal my whole walk. I normally just jot down the main gist so I can recall my conversation with God. I got carried away with that one year, and I spent a lot of time writing lengthy entries. One day I "threw away" the Sunday paper that was on the counter. Yeah, you guessed it. My journal went out with it. I was distraught. As I was pacing around thinking about my loss, the Holy Spirit said to me in a chastising tone, "I hate your journals." I knew immediately why the Spirit said it. I had let the content of my journals become an idol.

Maybe your role in your home has become an idol in your life? Are you always the victim, the teacher, the peacemaker, the breadwinner, the relationship fixer, the cheerer-upper, the attacker, the go-to gal, the only one that can do it right, or the strong one? When we are healthy, we are balanced. We should never be the something all of the time.

CHILDREN IDOLS

I saved the shortest but most insidious idol of all for the Christian woman—her children. This vision is going to make this very clear to you of God's perspective on the position your children must take in your home. I had a friend who did all for her kids and expected very little from them. Her relationship with her husband was not good; so she poured all of her time, money, and energy into her kids. We had many discussions about this being out of God's order for her home, but she just did not want to see it. She chose to call it, "I just love my kids so much!"

One night she had a very vivid dream. She dreamt that her thirteen-year-old son and she were having a great time playing a board game. Her Bible was on the table next to them and her husband was in the recliner, reclining. All of a sudden her son leaned over and began kissing her. Then he started to kiss her passionately. She said, "No!" He just smiled at her. That morning she called me, horrified. God was showing her that she has an "incestuous" relationship with her kids. Sounds yuck, huh? But are you really "hearing" me? God's perspective—when we give our affection, friendship, and devotion first to our children—is that it is *incestuous*! Yuck, yuck, and double yuck! Hit your knees and get those babies down from that throne.

Will you go over and over this chapter with the Lord and rout out those idols? Are you already aware of what your idol is? Great! Now get rid of them. How? Just like in the Old Testament. Hunt them down, tear them down, smash them, burn them, and fall on your face (get the bawl towel) and *repent.*

Chapter 8

IS IT MEDICAL?

*S*ANDY WASN'T NEW to support groups like ours; she knew the ropes. She had been riding the I-am-so-bad-for-hating-my-husband-I-repent-I-will-stop merry-go-round for years. She knew "good" Christians should open up, say the right things, and quote a scripture. Share, draw 'em in, and seal it. Everyone will nod heads in agreement, and Sandy will be *right*. Tonight, falling right into correct form, Sandy, once again confessed her anger and her disappointment in men, God, and marriage overall. Always being the first one to step up to the plate, she shared easily and with transparency about *her* wounds from her husband, *her* fears from men, *her* anxieties, and the myriad of ways that *she* had been wronged.

We leaned in, giving her full attention. We held the quivering of our chins so as not to draw from this raw moment of hers. Some even dabbed at their eyes, the moisture of empathy for *her*. She spoke with great emotion and brokenness. En suite, she poured out appropriate scripture for the situation. Finally she spoke confidently of the beautiful, godly, flawless marriage she will have as she waits on the Lord to *change her husband.* Sandy concluded with her newfound "revelation." She emphatically stated, "I get it! I need to let go of my anger toward my husband, men, and God!" She decided to do that right there and then, in the name of Jesus. We got to the core of her wrong "belief" that if she let go of anger, her husband would go unpunished. Sandy's countenance changed as one does when you have had a huge burden lifted. Her sweet, tear-stained face softened, the brokenness complete. We bowed our heads, allowing her a moment to "let go."

Whew! We all leaned back into our seats, recovering from the great emotional roller coaster she had just taken us on. Mind you, we had jumped on freely many times before, allowing her to be the sole focal point of our time. Sandy's husband, Grant, bowed his head in shame as her pain flooded the room, almost palpable. Whispers of "thank You, Jesus" hung in the room in support of *her.* God bless her for her frankness—*always* the Sandy, *always* the sharer, *always* the confessor, *always, always, always.*

The room silent, Grant's head bowed in shame, slowly lifted. Turning his face towards his wife, the unimaginable happened. Grant spoke up. I repeat; Grant spoke up! Witnessing such an intimate, tender moment, the group ever so slightly averted their eyes. We waited for this "breakthrough moment" to come to a sweet resolution with her "newly set-free response" to him.

His eyes soft towards his wife, he shared his love (she twitched), his inadequacies (her eyes squinted), and failures with her (she began all-out flailing). In fact, did the back of her head just slam against the couch? Is her mouth agape like a Venus flytrap? Are her eyes in the back of her head? "Is it medical? Do we need to call 911? It is just too much for her poor, broken soul? Someone get help!" Grants eyes glaze over, his body deflates in on itself, and he closes back down—silent. Grant was done, defeated once again. Falling prey to the spirit of Ahab and Jezebel, this couple was stuck in the cycle of control and manipulation by Jezzy and ungodly submission by Ahab.

WHAT YOUR FACE IS SAYING

OK, so Sandy didn't really need an ambulance, but you get the picture. Sandy, open and committed, gave her anger to the Lord in word; yet, she forgot to tell her face and her body.

Is that you today? Have you acknowledged your need to forgive your husband and let go of the anger and bitterness but have forgotten to tell your face and body? Experts will tell you our body language many times speaks louder than our words. What is your body saying to your spouse? "I am open, available, and willing to listen?" Or are you saying, "Back off; I don't receive what you are saying. I am *not* willing."

We all know what these are. These "behaviors" are the *voice* to our anger. Not voicing our anger is not being set free from it if we are still manifesting it in other ways. Be honest. We are still punishing.

How do you punish? Let me count the ways. Is it the pursed lips or squinty eyes? They will stay there permanently after forty you know. (They will, too; trust me.) Maybe you are a foot stomper or a door slammer. Yeah, you didn't "say" anything in anger but the floor shakes either way. How about a voice manipulator; are you one of those? You know what I mean. You don't yell (God forbid), but your voice totally changes. Is it higher, lower, slower? Oh yeah, now you're hearing me. Oh, I forgot a good one; the one where you can talk but your teeth are totally still clenched together. You have to combine that one with pursed lips or it doesn't work very well. Maybe we should address sarcasm too. I like to call that sour-chasm. You think you're getting your point across without that old sin of anger, but you are underhandedly carving out a big old chasm between you and your spouse.

Speaking of your face, how about the eyeball roll thing? I have to tell you, I can just see Jezebel perfecting this one in a looking glass pond some-where in her youth. I wonder what it was like the first time she used it. Was it powerful, shocking, repulsive? Hmm, maybe we need to put the old eye-ball roll in a different context. Would you do that to the CEO you work for while she was giving you a constructive criticism or to the slow receptionist at the return counter? Or, no, try this one; when your pastor is speaking an admonishment of the Lord over you? OK, I think you get my point. You *know* what you are saying with the eyeball roll. Be honest. I can *hear* your eyes speaking to your mate: "Whatever," or, "I am so sick of hearing this," or, "Will this ever change?" or, "Unbelievable, you are sick," or, "That is *so* your dad."

Now don't forget that brow. Those totally "unin-tentional" things that your brows do *can* be helped. I actually considered having Botox for that issue. One less thing I have to work on, right? Here's my deal; my sweet darling starts to wax eloquent about something that I know he has not prayed about (because I know all things) and I give him my full attention. No, really, I do; OK, I start to. I make eye contact, put down my Bible, lay my palms up and open, ready to "hear." His big plans are interesting, innovating...and *stupid*! What is he thinking (buggy eyeballs)? Is he really serious (frown in the brow)? Then he says," What do you think, honey?" So I'm thinking, "What do you mean, 'what do I *think*?' Did you not see my eyeballs and my eye-brows? Do you not see those same brows unfurling and shooting up like the golden arches right now? Like, do you not know that means? Are you *crazy*?" I knew you'd get that; I'll say no more. When I look at that picture from the outside, I can certainly understand why my sweet guy isn't just jumping right in for conversation.

TEARS

Another really effective conversation closer for men is the almighty tears. The reality is the Lord gave us tears for many healthy things like mourning, pain, great joy, cleansing, healing, etc. If you find yourself crying at every confrontation, it may be time for you to take a ride down "big girl" lane. There is a very fine line with this subject, and I certainly do not want to keep anyone suppressed. I remember a time when I was the one who was unable to have any kind of negative conversation without crying. It would, ultimately, stop our communication when my husband would say, "Please don't cry. I hate when you cry." The conversation would end and we would have no resolution. If you *always* have elevated emotions, please get before the Lord and ask Him to show you why you are so emotional. It may be that you have some severe wounds you need prayer, healing, and mentoring for. Or, you may have just not matured and honed your conflict skills. Or, possibly, the enemy is wreaking havoc in your mind. But, for sake of this topic, we will look at tears as a body language.

As I looked into my own "tearing" issues when in conflict, I realized that my emotional response of crying was because I felt rejected for not being heard or understood. When I was frustrated, I cried. When I was angry, I cried. When I felt "unheard," I cried. See the pattern? Well, sweet thing, guess what? When I looked at that pattern through the filter of *truth*, I began to put true words to the real emotions. I had to ask some hard questions. I said things like, "Lord, why did I cry in that argument. I wasn't sad." He replied, "Jamie, you were frustrated." Now I can say, "That is really frustrating to me. I feel like I'm not being heard right now." I can do it with *zero* tears. I learned to use *words* instead of tears to share my feelings.

Again, I am *not* saying that you should not cry when in conflict. I *am* saying you need to look at the tears and know *why* they exist in conflict so you can communicate clearly. I had to take that stroll down big girl lane and teach myself, with the direction of the Holy Spirit, how to communicate with words, not emotions.

Some of you are guilty of actual manipulation with tears. When you were a little girl, you got your way when you cried. You may have gotten attention with tears. Maybe you even changed the whole tone of your house if you cried. The end result, no matter your intention, worked for you. This is, like I said, a great manipulation if you use tears purposely to gain your own way or control the direction in a situation. It is deceitful. I pray if this is you, you will get real before the Lord and repent and stop it.

POSTURING

Here's one of my favorites—posturing. There's the lifting the chin or the jerking the neck to the side or the flipping of the hair. What do they mean? Maybe "I don't care," or, "Don't mess with me," or, "Try it, buddy, bring it on." If we posture, we *know* we are posturing. Are you a hands-on-my-hips girl? We have all seen men use the arms-over-the-chest thing, but the old hip one seems to be pretty much ours. Let us take a little journey down the birth of that baby.

Janie was four years old when she discovered that her momma looked one way in the morning rolling out of bed and another way when she exited the bathroom several minutes later. One day Janie decided to check that phenomenon out. She peeked through the crack in the bathroom door and saw Momma putting on that smile with a very magical "marker." When Momma left the bathroom, Janie slipped in, found that special "marker" and *voilà*, she sported that same pink-lipped smile Momma had. Hers, however, was to a much broader degree, like *much* broader. Delighted with her little self, Janie heard Momma coming near. Janie turned, grinning from ear to ear (literally). Momma gasped, frowned, leaned over, and *put her hands on her hips*. You know the rest of the story. That was power! She hadn't even said a word and Janie *knew* she was in trouble.

There is power in that hands-on-hips gesture of ours ladies. When we put our hands up there, it speaks a whole language of its own—powerful, unmovable posture. Moreover, our memories of the hands-on-the-hips maneuver are primarily of our mommas. Is that really how we want to be perceived by our lover, our friend, our husband? I would hope not.

THE TONE OF VOICE, OR NOT

Another affliction that masks overt anger is "I'm not listening/I'm not speaking." You *know* what I'm talking about. Maybe not you but you know someone who has this horrible affliction. I am afraid it is a double-edged affliction. A woman will be in "discussion" with her husband. He is just on the threshold of dangerous territory so carefully inquires, "I was just wondering (um); the department store bill came today with a charge on it I (um), didn't know about." Then you see it; her index fingers start to stick up, they slowly elevate, and the next thing you know, they are in her ears. (This is not in the flesh, of course, because that would be so-not-godly.) "I don't hear you. In fact, I so don't hear you that *now I can't speak.*" Not really, though; she *won't* speak. She has gone into full-blown I'm not listening/I'm not speaking-ism. This one is possibly the most insidious, as it is invisible. At least with a full-on medical emergency or head posturing or hands-on-hips, a guy knows what's up. Not so with the affliction of I'm not listening/I'm not speaking.

Ms. I'm not listening/I'm not speaking plays on the weakest part of a man—the missing "he should know" link. He doesn't even know he is missing it, ladies. So on goes the dance: he speaks and hurts you; you put fingers in ears and don't speak; he guesses and guesses and then guesses again, until, finally, *jackpot*! Yes, ladies, he "guesses" what the real issue is (the purchase was a sexy lingerie surprise). And *then* and only then, we speak. The funny thing is, now that he has "guessed" the right thing, our first words spoken in hours, days, or weeks aren't, "Yes, honey, that is it. You *do* know why I didn't tell you." Instead, they something like this: "You ruined my surprise. You don't even care. You don't understand me. You don't trust me. Blah, blah, blah."

Now the opposites of that, of course, are Sarah screamer, Yvette yeller, and Alice acidic. I can't believe I need to address this with women who love the Lord, but I have experienced it myself and I see (hear) it all the time. I want you to know I really do understand that many times it "seems" he won't listen unless you scream or hiss. But, God! But God is watching and listening, sister; this is His son, your husband. You are accountable to the Lord for the tone that you use with your husband. Really, if Christ were in the room, in his skin, would you yell at your husband?

Here is a little reality check for you. If you have a little boy, go look at him right now. Go! Lay down this book and go look at his precious little self (even if he is sixteen). OK, are you back? Now I want you to think about your tone of voice when you yell at your husband. I will tell you, *you* are exampling this behavior to your son. Your message to him is this: "It is OK for women to speak to men like this. Therefore, it is normal if your future wife speaks to you this way." Picture him standing before his wife and her yelling at him. Are you OK with that? I hope not. I pray the Lord will magnify your very own voice in your ear and you become acutely aware of how you sound when you yell or use a disrespectful tone with your husband.

Speaking of yelling, do you live next door to a woman that "barks"? I have to believe that she really cannot control her mouth. You can hear the *same* word over and over. She can be in the, kitchen, car, garden, pool, even in the bathroom, and there it is. She *barks* his name, "Josh!" Then you hear it louder, "JOSH!" Then it gets longer, "JAAASH!" And then it turns into several words, "JAAASH...UUU...AAAH!" You are either laughing or crying right now; laughing because you know her, crying because she lives next door to you, or crying because it *is* you. Come on now, it is, isn't it? And folks cannot fathom why you would choose to go through life "barking" at people, especially your husband. This is so unattractive, ladies; and, honestly, it gives us all a bad name. Would you yell at your boss from another room? Would you please just stop, leave the room you are in, and go *find* him if you would like to speak to him? Please? In fact, I dare you to call him "honey" or some cute thing when you find him. A sweet greeting can lift him up and make him way more receptive to you and your needs.

I don't know the areas you are using your body language in a disrespectful way with your husband. Maybe you are a stomper, a pouter, or a blaster. I would ask you to "go there" with the Lord yourself. Ask Him specifically to help you be aware of a tone, gesture, or anything that is dishonoring to your husband and, ultimately, to Him. He will show you the ways you are sending disapproving, angry, and judgmental messages in your body language. He will also show you the ways you can bless your husband with your body language. A touch, smile, or tender request will minister love.

Chapter 9

DIE, ALREADY!

So, I'M PROPPED up in my bed, fluffy pillows surrounding me, reading my bedtime story. Ugh! I read some more. Double ugh! I try to read some more. Ugh! Yikes! I rest my head back against the wall. Relax, breath, relax. "Lord, am I choking? What is going on?" With my eyes closed, I tried to relax. I feel my throat tighten more and the sense of squeezing intensifies. My mind's eye begins to see a picture of myself propped up in bed, and I see "it." "It" is a noose! Around my neck! Tightening! I can see the rope going from my neck and up the side of my face.

My mind is racing. "Lord, am I suicidal? Does the enemy want to kill me? Lord, what is going on?" I am about to rebuke the enemy when the Spirit says to me, "Jamie, look closer." With my eyes still shut, I pan out. There I am; propped up on pillows in my bed with a noose around my neck. My eyes search for the end of the rope. What? I see the end of the rope. Someone is holding it just above my head. I look closer. It's *me*! *I* have the end of the rope, and I am pulling *hard*! As soon as I see the whole picture—me sitting in bed propped up on pillow with a noose around my neck tightening at my own hand—the Holy Spirit says to me, "So, would you die, already?" "What!" I retort. He repeats, "Would you *die*, already?"

The movie in my head starts to play. When my husband asked me to vacuum the boat on a certain day, did I? When the Holy Spirit told me to say that word of encouragement, did I? When my husband asked me to let something go, did I? Am I stomping around in my heart because things are not as they "should be"?

But God! But, but, but, butt—Bill E. Goat!

After the Lord and I had a good cry over my sin, we had a good laugh. I kept looking back at that picture in my bed with *me* hanging on to the noose. What a precious God. He allowed me to choose. Pull on that noose and *die*, already—or not. I had the choice to drop that rope and continue to minister to myself. I delight in the way my Father speaks to me. He is funny sometimes.

AREAS TO DIE

The Word asks us to *die to self.* (See Matthew 16:25; Luke 17:33; Romans 12:1; Galatians 2:20; 5:24; Colossians 3:3.) Will you take a moment and ask your King to show you the areas in your marriage that you need to die to you? I am either a yes or a no; *you* are either a yes or a no. I can see now that I have been a "no" in many areas, subtle or overt.

Needs

One of those areas became clear to me one day when Katlyn and I were having a visit. I was sharing some of my "needs" in my marriage with her. She is always a good sounding board, is even tempered, and, for the most part, won't enter into my emotions. A few minutes after I hung up, she called me back. The caller ID revealed it was her again, and I answered the phone, "Hey, don't you hate when we talk that long and you still forget something?" Silence. "Katlyn, you there?" I had known her long enough to know the silence meant only two things. She was either bound with emotion and couldn't speak, or she had to say something to me that I was not going to like. This time it was, yeah, the latter. "Jamie," she carefully treads. "Will you ask the Lord if those 'needs' are really 'needs' or, are they 'desires'?"

You see, ladies, it is of the utmost importance that your friends are godly women who will seek Him on your behalf. My immediate response was, "No! I *need* him to blah, blah, blah. How can we have a marriage without blah, blah, blah?" Silence. Oh man, I just "heard" what I said. My precious friend "allows" me to let my own words sink in: "I need, need, need." Softly, Katlyn leads me, "Can you just let Him be that for you? Is He enough, Jamie? You have good, godly *desires*, but is it really a *need*?"

I got the towel. On the floor of my living room, we press through it, my King and me. "I need, I need, I need. Do I *really* need, Lord? What do I *need*? Doesn't the Word say that *You* are all that I need? Have I allowed the enemy to cloud the line between need and desire?" Why, yes, I have! I know that all I need is Him. And if I seek Him and tell Him my *desires*, He *will* answer me. I love that the answer might be a yes, no, or later; but it is *His* answer.

Expectations

Another area the enemy lies to us is the area of expectations. When we enter into a marriage we have a "picture" in our minds of how that will be. Will you take a minute or a thousand and talk to Him about that today? What well are you dipping in? We know from Scripture that Jezebel was dipping from a very evil well. Her well was against God and full of death, lust, control, manipulation, and self-prosperity.

I will tell you the well I was dipping from. He is handsome, hard working, kind, sensitive, godly, always even tempered, a martyr, the pillar of the community, full of integrity, a teacher of high standards, a very tender lover, and (I'm sure) in tune with his wife's every emotion. He always speaks in melodies, delights in *everything* his wife and children do, runs towards his wife (in slow motion), backs his wife up, and *loves* to have deep intimate conversations about love, life, and Jesus. Ah, yes; that is him! This is the well I was digging from— the Charles Ingalls well. Yeah, so that dates me. He was the *man*! That's right! The well in my real home life was not the total example for a young girl, but Charles was. Now that I think of it, my mom and I watched him together. I wonder if she longed for that same thing—for Charles Ingalls to walk in the door at five and be all things to her.

What is in your well? Where did it come from? Have you asked yourself where your expectations of marriage have come from? Are they realistic? Are they godly? Have you asked the Author of marriage to show you the template for marriage?

You see, when I placed all of these expectations on my husband, I set us up for failure. Let's look at how that might feel on the other foot. Your husband comes into your marriage with his well as a size zero (forever), double D, sex kitten, with the cooking skills of a chef who brings in six figures a year, loves fishing, keeps a pristine house, always responds "yes dear," never spends a dime, and adores the ground he walks on—always. How does that feel? Do you think *you* can fill those requirements? Yeah, not! We were not called to those things. Nor was your husband called to *your* expectations.

Arrogance

I want you to know that I am the last person who is going to excuse your husband's bad behavior. All I am asking is that you keep your eyes focused on the only thing you can change in your marriage— *you*. Isaiah 13:11 says, "I will punish the world for its evil, the wicked for their sins. I will put an end to the arrogance of the haughty and will humble the pride of the ruthless." Ladies, do you see the evil in hiding the new purse, hating him in your heart, being unforgiving or bitter, withholding the truth, pouting, shutting down, berating, screaming, and disobeying? These are sins, sister. Are you so arrogant that you think *you* know your husband's heart, motives, thoughts, and intents? Are you so haughty that you feel the need to *tell* him his motives, thoughts, and intentions?

The Lord sees those things that *both* of you do and do not do that are sin. He sees. He will show you your ways if you allow Him to. He will show your husband his ways too. Are you ready for the King to humble your pride or will you fall at His feet and humble yourself?

So you don't think you are haughty? Let me show you the ways. My husband is a perfectionist. He picks up after himself, sweeps things incessantly, puts things away, and stores his shoes with the laces inside so they don't get dirty on the floor. Yeah, I know; how can I complain? Well, let me restate that. My husband is a perfectionist. He picks up *my* stuff, sweeps *after* I already did, and puts *my* stuff where I don't know where to find it. And the laces thing—really? I'll buy new laces if they get soiled. So, one day I am whining at the Lord about this. Suddenly I "see" myself at a speaking engagement standing at the podium, and my husband is in the background, *sweeping*! The Holy Spirit lets me look at that for a moment and He says, "Jamie, don't quench Jim's need for detail. It will be for *your* benefit. I will use it for your ministry." I don't know if you know this, but the Lord *always* speaks the truth. The truth is that my husband's eye for detail and his perfectionism fill in areas where I lack. He is *the* greatest helper in my ministry.

I will have you know that I am so arrogant that I actually think I *know* how to read minds. Now, I am not talking about any spiritual gifts here. I am talking about the way that I (you) think we *know* our husbands' thoughts and motives. I had a life lesson one day as my husband shared with me an issue that was important to him. As he spoke, I am thinking, "You *mean* blah, blah, blah; you are *thinking* blah, blah, blah; and your *heart* is blah, blah, blah." Feeling incensed at the thought that he would *try* to manipulate his "true" meaning, I sarcastically asked, "Are you *saying* blah, blah, blah; *thinking* blah, blah, blah; and *feeling* blah, blah,

blah?" As I'm speaking I see this odd look on his face. Aha! Caught him in his own game, I did. I finish and he sits straight up. My normally slow-to-react husband blurts out, "No! Not at all! I am *hurt* that you think that of me. That is *not* what I meant *at all*! You don't know!" Wounded, he jumps out of his chair and storms outside, removing himself from my arrogance.

Let's look at what David had to say in Psalm 36:

> There is no fear of God before [her] eyes. For in [her] own eyes [she] flatters [herself] [knows everything] too much to detect or hate [her] [too busy looking at his] sin. The words of [her] mouth are wicked [harsh and condescending] and deceitful [speaking sweetly with wrong motives]; [she] has *ceased* to be wise and to do good.
> —PSALM 36:1–3, EMPHASIS ADDED

I ceased to be wise and do good to my very own husband. I wounded his spirit. I have the power even to kill his spirit. Jezebel brings death unto her own. I know absolutely *nothing*. No, I *do* know some things. I know that I am rebellious. We all are, just because we are human flesh—stinking flesh. I also know that God uses other's sin to refine us. Every time I will not die to the flesh, it ends up killing me anyway. When I won't "die," my spirit does, my emotions do, and my heart does. In essence, I really have no choice; either way, I experience death. I don't like this. *But*, one of them leads to life! I find that death to self goes much better when we let Jesus facilitate it. When we have gone past Him and His way of helping us die through obedience, it is then that we have to take the noose and pull hard.

Being a perfectionist usually goes hand in hand with control issues. Hence, my husband wrestles with control issues. One day after he told me how to, when to, and why to do something, I was particularly frustrated and *whining* to the Lord about it. I just have to stop here and thank Christ that He is long-suffering and merciful. Whew! Where was I? Oh, whining; "God, I can't take it anymore! Why won't You deal with his control issues?" The Holy Spirit, in the middle of my mini-tantrum says to me, "Jamie, I will leave it until *you die* to it. It remains *because of you*, not Jim." What? Why? Well, I will tell you why. The Lord can and will use other people's issues, and even sin, to prune you. At that point in our lives, my husband was choosing not to be set free from his controlling behavior, But God was using that very issue to teach *me* another area— to die to self. My "self" wanted to rebel against my husband "lording it over me." The truth is, the *only* Lord over me is Jesus. I can die to Jim because I have Him. My Daddy sees.

Speaking of the Father, I know by now that you are getting the picture that I spend a lot of time on the floor, face in towel, bawling my head off before the Lord. It's the only way, sister. 1 Peter 5:7 says "Cast all your anxiety on *him* because *he* cares for you" (emphasis added). That is what I do down there

on my carpet with my towel and my Word. I cast
on Him; I throw on Him; I pound the floor, scream,
cry, and have little flailing fits. You get the picture.
He knows what is in your heart; even the really ugly
stuff. Just say it. Just do it. Cry out to Him. He will
meet you there in your brokenness. He meets me.
He met me.

One particular day I was there. It was one of the
really "good" ones. I won't say they are bad. Bad
comes to no good. Good comes to freedom. So, I
am on the floor, face down in my bawl towel, and I
am almost "bawled out." I have, reluctantly, "died"
at the request of my King that day. Moaning lightly
now, as the big stuff has knocked the fleshy fight
right out of me, with eyes closed, I "sense" something directly in front of me. In my mind's eye, I
lift my head and I see. I see sweaty, dirty, bare feet.
My eyes travel up man legs trickling with dusty
sweat and then to a chest—sweaty, dirty, bloody,
and heaving—with His nailed-down arms stretched
wide. And His face; oh, dear Jesus, His face—thorn-
crowned face—blood, dirt, and sweat running
down my King's face. His head hanging, nailed to
that cross, His face over me. And His eyes—His
eyes great pools of dark sorrow and love. He speaks,
"Jamie, is what I ask of you too much?" My heart
tore, like the veil, in an impossible way. It felt like
the actual tissue of my fleshy heart was ripped in
two and broken, yet not beyond repair. The Lord
broke my heart that day. He broke it unto Him unto
a most humble place. My Christ and my Savior gave

His life; could I *not* give mine and my petty "stuff"? Oh flesh, that you would only die!

I will not tell you the issue He laid before me that day. It is for my King and me. What will it be for you and your king? Is He your King? Are you your king, sweet Jezzy? Will you go there with me? What huge thing has God asked you *to do* or what has He asked you *not to do* in your marriage? Will you picture yourself there on the floor? Or, better yet, will you put this book down and get before Him right now? Oh, I pray that you do. Bless you for your willingness. He is faithful. He *will* meet you.

Chapter 10

Obedience: His Way or My Way?

I was going to put this chapter at the beginning of the book, but I was concerned that those of you struggling with Ms. Jezzy syndrome would have put the book down and walked away or maybe given it to someone who "really" has this problem. Ha! Now that the Lord has convicted you in one or many areas you may be wrestling with the Jezz, maybe now you will be willing to listen up a bit. This is hard stuff, but you will not be victorious over a spirit of Jezebel without the Holy Spirit. Without the Word of God in your spirit, you cannot obey those things of the Lord that will give you the victory.

I am not going to do an in-depth theological study on all of the scripture on obedience. I am going to share some scriptures that have been breakthrough stuff for me *when* I have obeyed it. Yes, I just said that. I do not always obey. Why do you think I can write a book on this subject? Not because of my expertise in it, but because of my struggles, failures, and victories with it. *When I obey the Lord, I can do all things.*

You will see *victories* in your walk and your marriage as you obey Him. Notice I didn't say *victory.* We are all going to go to our graves with areas in our lives that have not had the completed work done in our marriages or ourselves. This is because when we die, we will still be flesh. Where there is flesh, there is stinking. Let's talk about His way, and then we will take a look at my way.

Of course, one of the most important scriptures on love I have already shared from 1 Corinthians 13. You know the one, "Love is patient" (v. 4). I hope you have been doing a checklist in that area every day since starting this book. "Am I patient, kind, etc., with my husband, Lord?" Only you know the truth to that.

One day I was on the phone with a very close Christian friend. I was about to tell her something about my husband that was not edifying or uplifting at all. I chose *not* to filter it through my own criteria you will see in "Speaking the Truth in Love," chapter 11. My motive for sharing was to "out" his bad behavior and get a little "girlfriend" sympathy. I was just about to go into my tirade when the line disconnected. Just out of the blue. Now, ladies, this was years before cell phones so a "dropped call" is not what was going on. All I heard in my spirit was, "You *will not!*"

Remember Proverbs 14:1? "A wise woman *builds* her house, but with her own hands the foolish one *tears hers down*" (emphasis added). Ouch! If that one doesn't get your attention, try this one: Galatians 5:15: "If you keep on biting and devouring each other, watch out or you will be destroyed by each other."

We run here and there looking for power—power to change our marriages and power to change our husbands. Ultimately, you already posses that power! Your behavior and vocabulary have the power to change him, you, and your marriage. You can believe the Word and obey, or not.

I wonder how many times God has protected you from divorce? I know you might be saying, "That's protection?" Yes, it is, honey pie; yes it is. God hates divorce (Mal. 2:16). God does not hate divorced people, but He hates divorce. I think we would agree that we do too. Nobody is clapping and shouting, "Oh, goody! I hope someday after I get married, I get to get divorced." Remember my counseling session with my pastor from the first chapter? I was so sure he was going to "let" me divorce my unbelieving husband. Not so much! I praise God now that He intervened and stopped me from that path.

I laid that down for almost two decades until I "entertained" the thoughts once again. When things got more difficult than I could imagine, yet again, God showed me divorce was really not my desire at all. The Lord gave me 2 Timothy 2:3–4 at that very time: "Endure hardship with us like a good soldier of Christ Jesus. No one serving as a soldier gets involved with civilian affairs—he wants to please his commanding officer." I *am* a soldier of Christ. I do *not* want a divorce; I *do* want to please Him. All we need to do is ask Him for our marching orders.

Maybe you are not being honest with *you*. You see in 1 John 2:9 the Word says, "Anyone who claims to be in the light but hates his brother is still in the darkness." Are you in the darkness, precious? I was in the darkness. I "thought" I hated my husband; I entertained hateful thoughts against him. Then I had a sister in the Lord come to me. She approached me with fear and trepidation. Really, she did! Can you imagine having to go to a friend with this word: "Jamie, the Lord told me you need to have compassion on Jim; you have no idea what is in his heart." Then you pause and continue: "James 3:16 says 'For where you have envy and selfish ambition, there you will find disorder and very evil practice.'" Yikes!

When I shared in chapter 3 how I went my own way, you learned how *I* was chasing after what *I* wanted. As wonderful the motive might have been, I was choosing, controlling, forcing, and going *my* way in *my* time. I was out of order in my own home. I was out of God's order. The Word says my husband is the ordained head of my household. I either believe that is the truth or not. If I do not believe it, I am in the *sin of unbelief.* If I do not obey it, I am in *disobedience.* If my husband does not believe it or obey it, *he* is in unbelief or disobedience. I, in that case, still have the power to change my home through prayer for him in those areas. Colossians 4 tells us to "devote yourselves to prayer, being watchful and thankful" (v. 2), and later in the chapter it says, "Always wrestling…for you" (v. 12).

God's way is humble and gentle. God's way is healing and forgiving. We will stand before the Lord alone, ladies, not married. God tells us in His Word what He wants of us:

> As God's chosen people, holy and dearly loved, clothe yourselves with *compassion, kindness, humility, gentleness* and *patience. Bear with each other* and *forgive* whatever grievances you may have against one another. Forgive as the Lord forgave us. And over all these virtues *put on love*, which binds them all together in perfect unity.
> —COLOSSIANS 3:12–14, EMPHASIS ADDED

We will, or we won't.

Where has your disobedience taken you? Mine has taken me down some pretty nasty paths, ladies.

I dare you to take a look at where you have chosen to run with sin against your husband and your God. In fact, let's play this show-and-tell game. I will show you my sin if you show me yours. How many times have you had a conversation with a good gal pal about how you have sinned against your man? Never? Well, today is your lucky day. I am going to share with you, and then you are going to tell me, a close friend, and God what you have done. It is called confession, sweet thing. Here goes:

OK, so, I was *really* mad at God. I was being "nice" for a very long time and it *didn't work*! My husband was still mean and distant. So my journal entry goes like this, "It is my anniversary today, Lord, and I am so mad I could just spew a really bad word. I am angry, angry, angry at the nothingness in our relationship, I feel nothing towards Jim, his presence irks me. I hate *me*. I don't want to spend time with You, God. And [really bad word] on it sounds *really* good to me right now. Argh! How's that for truth, Lord?" I am beginning to figure out when you talk to the Lord, He talks back, even when you do not want to hear what He has to say. Maybe I will try the silent treatment next time. (You get that's a joke, right?) So my sweet Jesus takes me to Hosea 13 and 14. Go read them. Ask yourself if this is you and God pertaining to your marriage.

When I was letting my marriage be the king in my life, I was not calling to the Lord; so God deals with me (13), and then our precious Savior gives, and gives, and gives again (14). My way stinks.

Oh, I found a few prevailing themes about myself in my journals:

1. Expectations are pride; who am I to decide how all things should be?

2. "He should know" is judgment pride.

3. Judgment against him is pride.

4. Bitterness and unforgiveness are revenge.

5. Intolerance is rebellion.

6. Unwillingness is a kinder word for disobedience.

7. My tongue has its own demon.

8. The demon in my tongue is powered by the one in my mind.

9. When I fix He won't; God is a gentleman.

I have mentioned physical affliction as a way the Lord allows our own sin to be revealed. Do you want to try this one? For six months my tailbone hurt so badly that I had to sit on one cheek to bear sitting down at all. I had sisters in the Lord pray for me. As they prayed for me, the Lord revealed once again that I had gone to a very unforgiving, hardened place with my husband and my in-laws. Amos 1:11–12 says, "Because [she] pursued [her] brother with a sword, stifling all compassion, because [her] anger raged continually and [her] fury flamed unchecked, I will send fire on [her]." Yes, ma'am! I had fire down there. I repented and the pain was gone.

One of the worst times of physical affliction for me led me to the following scripture and understanding. The scripture was Isaiah 1:5–6: "Why should you be beaten anymore? [I had several afflictions at one time.] Why do you persist in rebellion? [This was why I was under the heavy hand of God.] Your whole head is injured [I was having headaches], your whole heart afflicted [I had just found out I had a heart defect and was having chest pains]. From the sole of your foot [I had just had foot surgery and was in terrible pain] to the top of your head there is no soundness [I felt I had no peace in my mind]—only wounds and welts and open sores [I had a sore on my mouth]." I was in the *pit* of physical affliction, sisters. I would hate to find out that you have been suffering consequences of sin and were not even aware of it.

There is a way out. Will you ask Him, if you have an affliction right now, if there is a *spiritual* reason? Do you think a physical affliction in the spirit realm has to look a certain way? No. Can a stiff neck tell you that are being stiff-necked unto the Lord? Can an aching back tell you that you are carrying burdens God never asked you to carry? How about that sore on your tongue? Have you been speaking vile things? Is there a recurring physical something in your life? Maybe it is an affliction for revelation. Ask Him.

Idolatry is disobedience. Have you ever noticed how other people can say or do things to you and you are able to leave the issue alone, forgive it immediately, or confront it with kindness; yet you are unable to do the same for your spouse? Why is that? I was pondering that before the Lord one day. I realized only my husband offended me. When people are nasty to me, I am generally able to filter it through my Jesus. My self talk might go something like this, "Gosh, Lord, she was really rude to me. I forgive her and I ask that you bless her and touch her heart today. Help heal her and set her free from anger." I am constantly filtering people's bad behavior through mercy and grace. Not so much for my man. So the Lord had a little chat with me, "Jamie, when others hurt you, you are able to 'see' their sin as simply that—sin. You forgive their sin because you realize you are no different than them, a sinner. You do not *allow* your husband the same opportunity. Your husband is a sinner. You make your husband's sin about *you*, not him. His sin is his sin. It should not affect you; it is *his*."

Your husband affects you because you make the sin (his anger or control) about *you*. That means when he is impatient, *you* are wounded; when he doesn't do something for you, *you* feel devalued; or if he doesn't say something just right, *you* don't feel cherished. I am not saying these things are OK. I am saying that we need to filter them for our husbands the same way we do for others. My self dialogue was, "He is mean to *me*; I'm not good enough, and he is rejecting *me.*" See the "me" in there? I was filtering his sin through *me* and filtering other people's sin through Christ. Nice, real nice. I had put my husband in a place of higher expectations than others. Well, let me tell you; I took him down really quick. Really, I did. I had him such a high place with such high expectations that he was over God to me and not under the grace of God. Wow!

Enough of my disobedience, I have already divulged too much of *my* character.

Our precious Savior has given us the way of forgiveness and healing. Do you feel like there is no movement in your marriage and that God has stopped showing you the way to go? If that is you, will you go back to the last time He gave you instruction? What did He ask you to do? What did He ask you to stop? It may be the last place you disobeyed Him that you stalled out. I have found that my Father does not give me instruction number four until I have walked out numbers one through three. He may be waiting for *you* to move, not your spouse.

The Lord asked me the most precious thing the other day. He said "Jamie, I want you to be a gentle breeze to Jim." Wow! I allowed the Lord to help me to "see" what that would look like. The gentle breeze was quiet, kind, comforting, fresh, and new. You see, He doesn't ask us to walk in anything we have not experienced. Anything we are asked to do, we have the cross of Christ available to us. So, I forgave my husband, again. He looked at me and asked, "How do you do that? Are you really that stupid, or are you really that forgiving?" I responded, "Jim, I must obey the Lord. When I don't forgive you, it makes me very icky."

My darling dolls, you see; obedience is all about you.

> Let us not become weary in doing good, for at the proper time we will reap a harvest if we do not give up.
>
> —GALATIANS 6:9

Chapter 11

SPEAKING THE TRUTH IN LOVE

 OU ARE MEAN!" I cried with all honesty.

I had spent many years walking on eggshells, covering my heart with a huge brick wall, and not allowing Jim's behavior to affect my emotions. But now I knew Jesus. I had wrestled for many days with my emotions. His behavior lately had been extremely hurtful. I had some newly found Christian teachings to funnel my thoughts through. Let's see: I am *not* supposed to *lie*, I *am* supposed to speak *kindly* to my husband, and I am also supposed to speak the *truth, in love*. "This is very confusing, Lord." So I did what every believer does; I sought the Lord. I asked Him to speak to me about what I should or should not say to my husband and when it should be done. Then I waited and trusted God to do it.

When my husband walked in the door at lunchtime, I was not aware that it was the very time God chose. He had hardly gotten in the house when he spoke out a not-so-very-nice thing. Then the Lord did such a precious thing in me. He opened a deep well in me. The pain I felt was so powerful, so deep and searing. The tears came with the pain. I was so hurt that I sat down at the table, put my hands over my face and *howled*! Yep, I did. I didn't even have time to seek the Lord when I cried out, "You are mean, mean, *mean*!" I will never forget the look on his face.

Before knowing Jesus, my favorite name for him was "jerk." That word, I know now, only put him on the defensive and gave him shame about *what* he was. It was intended to hurt him. Today was different. I had never used the word *mean* with him before. The word explained his *behavior*, not *what* he was. Even though I was young, I almost felt foolish and immature when the word came out. He stood there, that look on his face, and wept. He sat at the table with me, and when I had released all the pain to the Lord, I spoke. It was rich, sister. The entry in my journal that day so long ago reads like this:

> I have finally let someone besides Jesus see my heart. I broke today. I shared my broken heart

with Jim. I was open, vulnerable, and humbled before him. I am so wounded when he is mean. "Lord, I can't be 'tough' anymore." This is so painful; but right. We cried together. "Thank You, Lord; *You helped me to speak the truth.*"

You see, my precious sweet things, I was always funny, happy, strong Jamie. I was the one people came to in crisis. I was the one who laughed off my issues. I was the one who didn't share about the emotional abuse because "Christian" women don't do that. Besides that, Jim was very good at hiding his behavior; and, because I had such a strong (not quiet and meek) personality, people just thought I was being a "Jezebel." Wow, that makes you want to speak up, huh?

Before I go on I want to address a couple things that you can take to the Lord and see what He says to you about them. The first one is what I call the "Christian gag order." I believe if we take the *full* context *and* Jesus' example, we *are* to speak the truth in love. So I am going to give you criteria that I feel will give you the freedom to share your struggles. When you share your marital struggles with others:

- Check your motive. Are you sharing just to expose your mate's behavior (which you should if it is abusive in any way) or are you sharing for the express purpose of receiving wise counsel for your issues?

- Have you chosen a godly, trustworthy, mature-in-the-Lord person to share with?

- Is this someone who can love your spouse no matter what they know about him?

- The Lord desires you to always run to Him first; have you done all that you can do, with the Lord, to get through this issue?

If you are bothered by these points, please remember what the Word says about wise counsel, going to leaders when someone has offended you or is in sin and will not heed, and speaking the *truth*. When we put a gag order on women, we are removing a godly venue where she can come, express the truth, and bring to light issues that may bring life (with wise counsel) or death (without wise counsel) to her, her marriage, her children, and/or her husband, . If we do not allow a safe place to speak the truth, we are setting couples up for a possible place of darkness in their marriage. How many Christian women have you met that have suffered years with an alcoholic or a mental, verbal, sexual, physical, or spiritual abuser? Too many, ladies, too many! I must reiterate, at this point, that this can be seen in reversal in a marriage; men can suffer at the hindrance of a gag order also.

This leads me to my next area. It really is about an area too. In my state we call this phenomenon "Minnesota Nice." We even have a restaurant by that name in my homctown. Seriously, we do. Now if you are not familiar with this, let me give you a little example. Comment: "I tried a new recipe with cloves in the pie; isn't it just decadent!" Nice but not true response: "Oh my yes, Doris, it is nearly the best (gag) thing (wretch) I have ever eaten." Or, how about this one? "Do these jeans make me look fat?" Nice but not true response: "Absolutely *not* (Are you kidding? It's like they're only two sizes too small!), Jenny, they are spectacular!" Now this is my very favorite: "Are you hurt that I didn't invite you to my B Well party?" Nice but not true response: "Oh no, Kim, I totally understand (I only cried for an hour)!" So, you get the drift, right?

I have a name for this: lying. Oh, my Christian friends, it is lying. Omitting is also lying. Now I know that these are really small things and we need to address the life changing stuff, but I really need you to "get" this. Do you understand that we are an example of Christ to the world; and if we cannot tell the truth in the things that are *little*, then how will we tell the truth in the things that are *huge*? A bigger thing would be informing your husband that his issues are too big for the two of you and he or both of you need to seek counsel, *even* if it makes him mad.

This "nice" thing is so prevalent in my state that I have, honestly, had to mentor women, Christian women, in the area of telling the truth. In case this is you (if you are from the East Coast, you can skip this part. You, my sisters, have a different issue; the "in love" part of speaking the truth in love. We will get to that.), let me just lead you through what the above interactions would look like if you chose not to lie: "Doris, you are such a great cook and I love when you try new recipes. I, however, would suggest you *do not* share this one with anyone." Then there is Jenny. (I have a prerequisite for anyone who is going to be my friend: tell me the truth. When I try things on, you *need* to be my honest critic. Save me from myself, please!) Anyway, a truthful response would be, "Jenny, I love you too much to suggest you wear that in public. If you adore it, wear it at home with no one there." And then to my favorite, "Kim, I obviously have some rejection and jealousy issues to work on. I *was* offended when you didn't invite me. Besides that, I really need some B Well products."

So are the latter or the first examples you? Aha! Liar, liar pants on fire! Now go put this book down and repent. First of all, you need to go to Jesus if you *are* offended all of the time. My friends do *not have to* invite me, sit by me, or caretake me. They are my friends, I trust them. If they do not want to invite me, they do not have to; no explanation needed, none of my business. Now that is freedom!

Speaking of repenting, I told you I would get back to you—my ladies from the East Coast that is. I have lived with you. I lived near the East Coast for a season, and I visit my daughter on the East Coast often. Some of you chicks can be *mean*! I mean, *mean*! I know; I am making a general, sweeping statement. I actually found it a bit refreshing, coming from the "don't-tell-the-truth" state. All I am going to say is that you must speak the truth in *love* with the leading of the Holy Spirit. He does *not* say, "Girl, you are fat and ugly," even if it *is* true. I love you; rein it in under Him, sisters.

In all seriousness, ladies, it is kind to speak the truth to one another *when* led by the Holy Spirit. I wrote in chapter 3, "Broken Like a Brick," how the Lord showed me that I could tell my husband about my hate towards his behavior by opening that door for me to speak it. My husband *needed* to hear that so he could really know what was going on in my heart and how his behavior was affecting our children and me. How can he grow if you will not tell him the truth?

Speaking of children, out of the mouth of babes, huh? I was talking to my girlfriend about a situation with her son. She was concerned because when they were driving through town, he noticed something and made a comment. He saw a woman walking down the sidewalk. She was very large and had a difficult time walking. He looked at his Mom and said, "She is very fat." Immediately his Mother reprimanded him, "Honey, that is not very nice to say."

He quickly snapped his head around to look at the woman again, as if to check to see if he had really seen what he had seen. Yes, indeed he had seen a very large woman struggling to walk down the sidewalk. "But, Mom, She *is* very fat; she can't even hardly walk," this four-year-old retorts. She reiterated that he had behaved badly. He hung his head, not understanding and they went on with their day. When she called me, I could tell she was torn. After she told me the story, I asked her, "Why do you think you are wrestling with reprimanding him?" "Well, because it was the truth!" she cried.

My point is this. Are some people tall? Are some people short? Are some people brown" Yep, yep, and yep. Can it be that we have gotten so politically correct that we cannot speak the truth anymore? I, actually, *know* that I am short. I also actually know that I am fat. Now some people would say, "Oh, Jamie, you are *not!*" But the chart says I am. My concern is that we have become a people like the Old Testament false prophets who said, "Peace, peace" when there was no peace (Jer. 6:14; 8:11; Ezek. 13:10). Have we created an atmosphere where we can live in denial? My friend's son didn't say anything maliciously. He said what he saw. Why don't we reprimand him when he says his mom is tall or that I am short? The truth is, we can teach our children and ourselves to speak the truth with true words that are not hurtful words.

I am certainly not advocating walking around blurting out everything that comes to mind. I *am* advocating telling others and myself the truth. "Iron sharpens iron" (Prov. 27:17) and "an honest answer is like a kiss" (24:26). I bless my friend that told me a quarter cup of creamer in my coffee is *not* OK. She was just being kind enough to confirm to me what the Lord had already been telling me.

My girlfriend and her husband were in counseling. Their communication skills were very low. Beth was frustrated when Lon did not listen to her. After sharing with the counselor for quite some time, he asked them to assess the following scenario: You are driving on a long trip. You pass a little diner and Beth comments about how cute it is and reports they also have cherry coke, her favorite. Lon responds with a noise and keeps driving. The counselor went on, "Tell me what just happened here?" Lon speaks up first, "Well, she saw a cute diner; she sees stuff like that because she likes quaint things and she really does like cherry coke. She was just sharing, I guess." Beth's eyes are bugging out of her head now. "What!" she screeches. "See, I told you! He doesn't listen to you either. All I wanted was a coke." The counselor had Beth repeat the scene. Then he asked her, "Beth, at what point did you 'ask' to stop and get a coke?" She began to blurt out, "When I pointed out they had cherry coke," but then she caught herself. After playing the scene over and over, they came to two conclusions. (1) Beth needed to learn to say what she wanted *clearly*. "Honey, there is an adorable diner. I would like to stop so I can grab a cherry coke." (2) Lon could help her to learn to speak the truth by asking her questions when she was not clear. "Are you saying you would like me to stop, dear? Because I would be glad to." The most precious example of speaking a hard truth and speaking it clearly came from my eight-year-old granddaughter. She is normally so self-enthralled that we wonder if she is even aware of "others." Well, she is. My daughter and I were trying to decide what would be on the menu for Christmas. My husband interjected several times from the other room. Exasperated by the interruptions and resenting his "controlling" even this, I discounted all of his ideas. My sweet little granddaughter walks into the room and says, "I think you guys need to respect Poppa." I am in utter shock. This little ribbon-twirling, bejeweled, dancing diva took time away from the full-length mirror to get involved. I was very interested to hear what she had perceived. "What do you mean, honey?" I asked. "Well," sweet little puddin' says, "when he talks you should do what he says. Not *all* the time; but, you know, some of the times." Off she trots, leaving us *all* speechless. If you knew my daughter and me, you would know a miracle has just taken place—yes, we are speechless. "Dear God. Have I stooped so low that you have to speak to me through a child? A self-indulged, in-her-own-world, unaffected by us child? Don't answer that, God; I get it." Speak the truth, baby, speak the truth; I hear you.

Some of the reasons we do not speak the truth are valid. Someone may be hostile and not open to "hear." Even then we can be honest. We might approach them with, "I am afraid you really don't want to hear right now and your hostility is not lending me a very safe place to share, so I am not going to share today." In this case, you have not let fear lead you; you have allowed truth to lead you. Another area, especially for women, is the area of control. Yes, I said control! Do you know that walking on eggshells is control? Yes, it is sister. If this is your internal dialogue, "I better not tell him, he will be so angry. He doesn't need to know, etc." then you are controlling whether the conversation will or will not happen. You have decided what will be said or not said.

Ultimately you are walking in fear and self-preservation. You don't want to deal with his anger, rejection, or victim mentality, so you make sure it doesn't happen by not allowing the conversation. God is in control, remember? You may have been lying by omission. If you are omitting information out of fear of his response, you are lying. If you are not telling him your true desires out of fear, he will not fill them. You are protecting yourself from disappointment but not allowing him opportunity to know you. We must begin to *allow* our husband's discomfort and anger.

Maybe you are not speaking the truth because you don't want to hurt him. Well, if you "get it" that speaking the truth is *kind*; then are you not being unkind by withholding? Let's filter this through the truth. If you have a sin in your life and the Lord asks you to bring the truth out "into the light," it is probably going to be painful. If you are withholding something, are you not, in fact, allowing that very thing to stay in the darkness? It will never change if you never tell him. Oh, and his feelings? Are you kidding me? How would you like it if Jesus did not show you your stuff because He didn't want to "hurt your feelings?" I bet it would hurt worse to die and stand before the King of glory with sin in your life you weren't even aware of.

We see some parallels there in chapter 4, "Emasculate." You can treat your husband like a man and facilitate freedom in him or you can "baby" him. How do you think he would really feel if he knew that you thought he was that weak? Ladies, when we protect our husbands from pain, we do them a disservice. Can you trust that your husband is a big enough boy to "handle" it? How many times has the Lord used pain to refine and grow you? Will you afford your husband the same opportunity to grow through the pain?

I had a hard thing to say to my husband. Our grown daughter and her family had been home for a visit. We had a fantastic time, with one exception—my husband. When the house got too full or babies cried, he just could not keep it together. He had been particularly inhospitable this time. I was so grieved at what had transpired. I went to my bedroom, got on my knees, and sought Him: "Lord, I am so grieved. Yet again, his anger has hurt our children. This anger issue is too big for us. Help me, Lord! What should I do?"

We were three months away from moving out of state. In movie fashion, the Lord gave me direction. The Lord was very clear and it was not about my husband. It was about me. I walked downstairs and declared, "Jim, I love you; but I cannot live this way anymore. Your anger is destroying this family. It must stop. I need you to get help; you have two weeks to find a counselor. If you do not, I will not move halfway across the country with an angry man." His jaw flexing, he says through clenched teeth, "Are you giving me an ultimatum?" Speaking the truth clearly and honestly, I said, "No, I am giving *me* an ultimatum. I have allowed this in my life for too long. If you choose no, I will need to go look for an apartment and enroll in college so I can support myself."

I waited for a response. Nothing. I went back up to my bedroom and praised the Lord for giving me the words and peace to speak them. The next morning I came downstairs. Jim was having a cup of coffee and gazing out the window. Turning his gaze to me, he says, "My appointment is tomorrow." His face was desperate, as if to say, "Please see that I am serious about getting help." I was so proud of him! He "heard" me, he didn't "react" in anger, and he called—not after two weeks, but immediately. Oh, praise God! I had learned a great lesson about speaking the truth to my husband.

When I got a call from a good friend, this lesson was fresh in my mind. Kristen and I were very good friends. We had been for years. I had been married a little over ten years longer than she and her husband had been. She would call often to "discuss" things going on in her marriage, as many of their issues were similar to ours. Her conversation that day was something like this: "When he talks to me like that I feel so devalued. I was devalued as a child, and he just opens those old wounds. I feel like I am living with my angry mother again. I don't know why he doesn't see it." This one-sided conversation went on for a good while. I listened, made a noise of acknowledgement now and then, took some mental notes, and finally stopped her.

I always keep a running dialogue with the Holy Spirit when I am talking to a friend about any issue that needs wisdom. The Holy Spirit said to me, "Ask her if she has told her husband any of this." So I did. I interrupted and said, "Kristen, have you shared any of this with Neal?" Silence. "Kristen?" Silence. Then she spoke a quiet, "No." I responded, "You need to share this with him *before* you share with me." You see, Kristen had not followed my rule number four. This is biblical. Seek *first* the kingdom of God and if someone offends you, go to them. (See Matthew 6:33; 18:15.) I knew that my rules were godly, and I felt like we had usurped her husband's position by sharing this intimate thing before he was aware of it. Does that make sense to you? Put that pump on the other foot. Would you like him to share an issue about you with his buddy before he shared with you? Yeah, I didn't think so.

Let's end this chapter with a little flip-flop. How about other people speaking the truth to you? Can you honestly say you are mature enough to let others speak truth into your life? Do a little soul searching before you answer that one, honey. You may think you are; but are you? I had a precious sister come to me recently. She asked me to tell her any area in her life that God was showing me she was "off." I said, with some trepidation, "OK." I knew in my spirit she was not ready, but I agreed, right?

The very next night she called and said how angry she was with her son. Not only had she said some pretty hard words to him, she had also hung up on him. As she was telling me the story, my heart became grieved. I prayed, "Well, Lord, she asked me; so cover me, I'm goin' in." "Brea, you know how you asked me to tell you the truth if I see something in your life that is not godly?" "Yes, do you see something?" she begged. "Actually, I do." I went in carefully; "When you speak to your son in that manner and hang up on him, it is a poor example to him of a Christian. I can't imagine hanging up on one of my daughters; they are my most cherished gifts in my life." The next day I got a text from Brea telling me how awful I was. I did not hear from her for a week. Oops, not ready. I love when my friends rebuke me. I will tell you I have a couple of them that say whatever they need to say to me, whether I like it or not. They love me enough to not let me stay the way I am.

We can't leave our husbands out of this part of the conversation. I made a slightly under-the-radar-not–so-nice comment to my husband one day. He looked at me with a "gotcha" face. "Well! I think *you* are a little bitter and angry," he gloated (my interpretation). Instead of anger or defensiveness, I felt that knife. You know; the double-edged sword of the Word: "In your anger do not sin" (Eph. 4:26), and "Get rid of all bitterness, rage and anger" (v. 31). "O Lord, I am so sorry. I repent." Can your husband speak the truth to you? Can he really; without any of your body language "medical symptoms" showing up? Can he? You don't have to tell me. Tell him. Tell your husband that you need to hear the truth from him as well as him from you. You can do it, gals. Give it a try. Put Jesus in charge of your mouth and you will be amazed at what you say.

Chapter 12

ῶHAT NOW?

CHOOSE LIFE

$\mathscr{C}$HOOSE YOU THIS day life or death (Deut. 30:19). It is that simple ladies. You are a *yes* or a *no*. If you have seen yourself anywhere in this book, you need to begin with repentance. I need you to understand that repentance and forgiveness are two different things. The Word tells us to repent—turn the other way (Acts 3:19). You cannot turn away from something you do not acknowledge in yourself. Admit the sin before the Lord. If you do not hate the sin (sometimes we kind of enjoy a certain sin and that is why we do it; it is fun or "feels" good), ask the Lord to help you to see the behavior as He does to grow to hate it. Then decide to repent. You will have to ask the Holy Spirit to convict you and strengthen you to stop that behavior. You cannot do it without Him. Then, ask the Lord to forgive you. You see, when we ask the lord to forgive us before we have repented, it is asking the King of kings to do His part first. Confess, repent, and be forgiven, sister. When you walk in this pattern, you *will* begin to heal.

GUARD YOUR HEART

I have gotten hard-hearted so many times in my marriage. I have walked several years with a heart of flesh and then I find myself struggling, once again, with a hard heart. I get hard-hearted when I am not giving my troubles to Him and when I am not forgiving my husband. These two things put me in what I call "shutdown mode" with the Lord. I still love Him but I spend very little time with Him. One day after a few months of this kind of relationship, the Lord said to me, "Jamie, when you get hard-hearted it is because you have not spent time with Me, shared your heart with Me, or given Me any time. This is just like what your husband does to you. Shall I punish *you* like you do to him when he behaves that way?" Wow! "No, Lord, I want You to give me grace and mercy and forgive me."

What then, do you do with your heart? You guard it. The Word says for us to guard our hearts (Prov. 4:23). When I asked the Lord to help me to understand that, He showed me a picture. I saw a heart beating. It was soft, pink, fleshy, and beating in a manner that exuded vibrant "life." Then the Lord told me to look closer. I "panned" in. There was a very thin silver "thread" going every which way around the heart. On closer inspection, the thread was actually a very strong silver metal. The metal protected the heart from mortal wounding, yet left enough to be "exposed" to love and to give life to others. Did you get that part? While we must guard our hearts, we must also allow it to be exposed to others for love and ministry. And we *will* get wounded but not mortally.

So now you know what to do with your heart. But what do you do with your behavior? First off, above all else, you must learn to hit your knees. I am not your answer. He is! The Holy Spirit longs to guide you. He is your answer to what path to follow. It will likely include seeking a godly counselor, finding mature people to mentor you, and being honest and transparent with your spouse. Some of you may need intervention for yourself or your spouse for addictions or you might need to call the police or your pastor. Only you and the Lord are the sure way to go.

Set Boundaries

Maybe you need to have an understanding of boundaries. There are books to read and other resources to tap into. Go digging! I have had so many women ask me what a healthy boundary might look like. These are small examples but will give you a little picture to look at.

My husband travels for his work. One time he had been gone for about ten days. When he got off of the plane, he called me and invited me to meet him for supper. I was excited to have a "date" with him and was anxious to catch up face-to-face. We met in the lobby and had a little giggle as it felt a tiny bit clandestine to meet this way. Since the restaurant was on his way home, it wouldn't have made sense for him to pick me up and go back again.

Our meal arrived and his cell phone rang. Yep, you heard me; his phone was on. He began to have a leisurely "chat" with his coworker with whom he had just spent ten days. I waited, ate, and waited. After about seven minutes, I said, "Lord, how would You have me respond to this?" Normally I would have been very angry and hurt, possibly with a tear in my eye. But I was able to filter it through the truth, not through emotions. The *truth* was that my husband was more interested in what his coworker had to say than being with me, so I let him be. I put my fork down, picked up my purse, and left. My husband hadn't even touched his food yet, so I supposed he would be a while. On the drive home I *decided* I would not entertain the issue anymore. I could be wounded, angry, and emotional; or I could allow my husband to suffer the consequences of his choice. He got to finish his dinner alone knowing that he had just done a very bad thing.

He came home about thirty minutes later. When he walked in the door, I had my just-for-him on and let him know how much I *missed* him. He opened his mouth to apologize and I told him to hush up. Later he did apologize and was in awe of how I had just "let it drop." I didn't let it drop. I *chose* not to participate in a cell phone date, *chose* to give it to Jesus, *chose* to forgive him, *chose* to not allow it to ruin our first night together in ten days, and *chose* to behave in a new way. Praise God for changed behavior! Does that help at all?

Maybe you have a husband who is a procrastinator and the sink is still leaking a year after you first asked him to fix it. It is time to confess: "Honey, I have harbored bitterness over the sink thing and I am sorry. Will you forgive me? I really want that fixed. Would you be open to giving me a date it is going to be done by? If that is not OK, I can get a plumber." You may be surprised; he may just confess that he feels inept at plumbing and would love for you to call someone. You see, a boundary is more about you than it is about him.

One of my favorites happened to me bazillion years ago, but was such a turning point in our marriage that I remember it to this day. We were on our two-week vacation at the lake. Whenever it rained we would stay in the camper and watch a movie. We had agreed we would take turns choosing the movie. It was my "turn." I chose a Christian production that had changed my life in a mighty way and I was excited to share it with my daughters, as they were getting older.

My husband had suffered for many years from what I call the "bully" pattern. He would let me choose something (dinner location, color of the couch, movie, whatever). But if he disagreed, he wouldn't say it outright; instead he would make a snide or underhanded comment. I would then get emotional, shut down, and do whatever it was to please him. Not so this time.

I announced the movie for the night. He looked at me and very aggressively reported, "If you are watching *that*, I am going to bed!" Aha, this time I was set free for I had been reading a Christian book on boundaries. The Lord had impressed upon me one of the teachings about taking your spouse's words literally and not receiving manipulation if that was how they communicated. I did *not* allow Jim's "push" to *shove* me. I looked at him and very nicely said, "OK." Then, turning to my daughters I said, "Ladies, Dad is going to bed and we are going to watch a movie!"

It was like the world came to a standstill. Remember, we are in a camper with three girls ages eleven, nine, and five. Wide-eyed, they look from him to me and me to him. I held his stare, but I held it with openness and kindness. I was honoring his no. His world and pattern crashing down on him, he asks incredulously, "You are *still* going to watch it?" I repeated his own words back to him in, again, a very kind manner: "Honey, you said if I was watching this, you would go to bed. I am fine with that. You do not have to watch it if you don't want to; but it is my night to choose and this is what I am choosing." He went to bed. The girls and I had popcorn, chocolate, and a fabulous time. Our pattern, after that night, began to break. I had allowed his bullying manner of communicating to control me in a very negative way.

WORK ON CHANGE

Sweet things, if something isn't working, work on *it*; work on change. If the way you are responding *always* ends up the same way, stop! It isn't working! If your marriage is in deep trouble, it is OK to insist on seeking help together. If he is a no, you still go. If he is an addict, release him to tell you *when* he is going to seek help, not *if*. Is that helping a little? Speaking the truth in a different way will sometimes change a whole pattern. If he always gets drunk at Tammy and Brent's house, you don't have to go there with him ever again. If he throws his golf clubs when you beat him (at golf), you can tell him you will be finding a new golf partner if he can't play nice. Follow through if he doesn't stop. Give him kudos if he plays nice, but don't hesitate to beat him. Referring back to chapter 11, "Speaking the Truth in Love," can help you in this area. You go girl, you *can* do this. Help your husband to have victory by responding like you never have.

We were able to purchase a lake home finally, after desiring one for many, many years. This was made possible by two things alone (after God): the crash of the housing market and because it was a "gut job." Yeah, this place was a disaster! After about a month of twelve-hour, hot, sweaty demolition days, my husband got very crabby. I normally would walk on eggshells, be offended, and detach until he was "finished." This particular day I felt the Lord tell me to go to him. I approached him and asked, "You OK?" (I have a little clue for you; don't ever ask someone if they are crabby. Have you ever noticed if someone asks you that question, the question itself makes you crabby? Yep; so I didn't ask him that.) He looks at me and says, "I think I am just having a pity party." I took my time, looked deep into this tired, defeated man's face. And, instead of bawling him out (like I'm tired too, you know) or giving him the old "count your blessings" speech, I smiled a *huge* smile, kissed him on the cheek, and said, "Well, stop it!" He was stunned. "Just like that?" he yelled after me. "Yup! Just like that!" I grinned. We had no big deal, no big discussion, no big battle. We were a big boy and girl. Ha! Take *that*, Satan!

LET GOD

Do you still think you know everything after reading this book? I am praying for you that you realize you know nothing. When we know that we know nothing, it opens our hearts to learn everything. Just when you think God is not working on your husband's heart, something happens. Or, you may not know but you find out much later that something was going on in your spouse. I have seen this too many times to mention. I also now realize this is the enemy putting those thoughts in your head about God not working and you have to tell the enemy to shut up.

I want to share one precious time. It was so out of the blue that I was amazed by the way the Lord works. For many weeks after it continued to give me hope for our family. My husband was a very detached father. His leftovers from a policeman dad and very religious and stoic mom had left him with no deep well of attachment to draw from—only rules, order, and shame. Once when he was being extra controlling, I asked the Lord for a reprieve; I just could not take it anymore. The next day my husband got called out on a one-week job. Thank You, Jesus, for time-outs.

Even more spectacular, I had asked the Lord to show my husband his controlling ways but to not use me for once. My husband called after about four days on the road. I answered the phone, and all he said was, "I am so sorry." Baffled, I asked, "Why?" I almost could hear him hang his head on the phone. "Jamie," he confessed, "I am working with one of the most controlling people I have ever met. If this is how it is for you, it has to be terrible." Oh, praise God from whom all blessings flow! Did I just hear that? Not only did I get a reprieve, the Lord allowed him to actually experience how it is for *me*. Isn't that rich?

On another issue, I had prayed for years Jim would open his heart to his now grown daughters. One evening we were watching the movie *My*

Dog Skip. To be honest with you, I thought it was touching but to this day cannot remember the gist of the movie. With the credits running at the end of the show, I turned to ask how he liked it. There he was, tears streaking his face. Being the sensitive girl I am, I said, "What the heck?" He could not speak for a few minutes. I quietly prayed for him. I was also thinking he was having a "my dog died when I was nine and I didn't get to say goodbye" moment. I waited. He looked at the floor and wept. I waited. Finally, he lifted his head. "I was such a rotten dad," he wept.

Ladies, this is where you *must* tell the truth. If you do not allow your husband to *feel* the truth, he cannot heal from it. I did *not* tell him he was a good dad. He was not. I held him. Finally, I said to him, "The Lord will forgive and so will your girls. Will *you* forgive you?" You *do not* know what God is up to—*really. My Dog Skip?* Really? Not long after that, my husband brought together his daughters and confessed, repented, and asked their forgiveness.

So the King forgives my husband. My children forgive their daddy. Now what? Deeper, deeper still. I'm in a new season, a season that has moved me far from my children and far from friends, family, and my church body. I am *feeling* very alone, angry, and lost. In violent, self-pity-filled prayer, I "see" a backhoe. It is one of those yellow ones, roaring with power and digging deeply. Dirt is falling from the scooper and I scan the picture to the operator's seat. And, there He is—my King, my Savior, my precious

Counselor and Friend. He is dredging away, having a ton of fun *in His robes.* (He is so weird with me like that sometimes.) Anyway, as I laughingly take it all in, I inquire of the Lord, "Lord! What is that?" Jesus looks at me and impishly says, "This is gonna stink!"

He is going to "dig it up" sisters, *if* you *let* Him. Here is where we went:

1. "Jamie, you are angry because you have not forgiven *yourself.*"

I needed to forgive myself for not doing all that I needed to do to help our marriage, not always being honest, not protecting my children, not, not, not. Then, I received that forgiveness from my Lord—forgiven. And if I am forgiven, then who am I to not forgive my husband?

Are you forgiven? Then who are you to not forgive? Forgive; every day forgive. Remember, forgiveness is forgiveness; trust is to be earned. Forgiveness and trust are two different things.

I saw my Jesus one day, drenched in blood. His wounds were mortal. I killed Him yet He forgave me.

2. Pride. "Jamie, you are so mad at Jim because he won't do what he is 'supposed' to do. *Nor* do you; but I have grace and mercy on you."

Ouch! The truth is, God sees what my husband does. I am in charge of me, my weaknesses, my faults. In fact, I am seeing that I have so many that I don't have time to worry about my husband's "stuff." "O Lord, forgive me—again!"

Will you let Him show you?

3. I cried out in this time, "O God! Change me!" He replied (in a silly, kind of mocking way), "Oh, Jamie! Obey Me!"

Is He the Lord in your heart, behavior, and emotions? Is He? Ask the Holy Spirit to enable you to obey.

4. I allow the Lord to dredge and dredge—stinky but healing.

Return to your leftovers, doll; return. Let the King of glory show you where old hurts are, where you need to forgive people in your past so they no longer control how you respond to your husband.

5. Many years ago my friend told me she "saw" my husband through the Lord's eyes. He was a toddler, a spiritual toddler. Today, through this dredging, I "see" my husband. He is a *teenager*! He *is* growing in the Lord, whether I think so or not.

Ask the Lord to let you see your husband the way He sees him.

6. I am filled with hate and malice at my husband, at my expectations not met in my marriage, and at my god. My "god" has been my marriage, always focused on "it."

Let it go, sweet things. Let "it" go, and let the King of glory be your God. What about you? Is God speaking to you? What is He telling you?

I remember one time when the Lord said to me, "Jamie, you are so busy looking at what he *isn't* that you miss seeing what he *is*." Or another time the Lord showed me that I simply was *not* casting my cares on Him every day (1 Pet. 5:7). Sweetheart, sometimes I have to go "tell" Jesus on my husband ten times in one day. After I tattle I then give the issue to the Lord and tell Him that I trust *Him*, not my husband. The Lord has asked me to treat my husband in a godly way no matter how I feel *or* what his response is. I know I must battle for my marriage. Satan would love to destroy us.

I was on my knees weeping for my marriage one day, and I saw a vision. Jesus walks over to me and holds out an empty silver platter. I knew He wanted me to lay my burdens on the platter, so I did. He turned to walk away and I could hear Him say, "I will take care of these." I must trust He is working for us. Will you kneel before your Savior and lay your burdens on that platter today? He longs to carry your burdens. Go, now!

Finishing Work

I have been away for a while. Yes, I have. You see, I don't ask you to do anything I haven't done or am not currently doing. This one took a couple hours. I just got off of the floor, honey. Yes I did. I still hit the floor. It is Him and it is life.

I had two people very close to me hurt me in a deep way today. I grabbed my Word and headed to my prayer closet, and I wept and wept. I held my Bible to my chest with a grip and gut-wrenching wail, "I will *not* let go of you, God! I am dying inside. I can't let go. I understand if I *do*, there is *no* hope for me."

He gave me a scripture that reminded me that He sits on the throne and sees what I am going through (Ps. 113:5–6). I stamped my feet and bawled through a "warring" praise and worship song; I *will* war through the pain. As I wretched with emotion, I heard His voice, "I am doing a finishing work. Do you want that?" I cried out, "Yes, Lord, I want a finished work!" I had no idea what that meant.

Then I fell; I fell to the floor and emptied my pain to Him. I emptied the pain of the rejection from these two people I love. I was there for a very long time. When the tears ebbed and the sobs becoming hiccupping sighs, I saw Him. His robes were coming closer to me there on the floor. And then He picked me up. He carried me like a tiny little girl. He carried me. I could see my feet hanging as he carried me like a child with a grave wound. And He sat. He sat on a park bench and held me in His arms. As I wept into His robes; the comfort flowed over and through me. He stroked my hair and kissed the top of my head.

The "finishing work," my precious dolls; the finishing work. People (even these two) are *only* people. They can do painful things to me, but they are not so important that they can destroy me. Christ has my heart because I have given Him all of my heart, soul, and mind. I have gotten to this place one piece of flesh at a time.

Will you let Him do the finishing work in your marriage? Will you? His covenant with us is forever. He will never leave you nor forsake you. Your covenant with your God and your husband are holy, immeasurably valuable, and precious.

What now, sisters? Go! Go to Him. He knows things about you that *you* don't even know. Be honest, be raw, be angry; just *be* with Him. He knows the secret, dirty, painful, hidden things of your heart.

Will you do this for me? I have bared my "ugly" for you and your marriage. Will you bare your "ugly" for your marriage? You may find out that your "ugly" has a name. Yup, you know it. Ms. Jezzy, it is time to go packin'! Disinvite her; no more dinner invitations. Kick her to the curb; divorce her!

Will you go to Him so the enemy cannot claim another Christian marriage? Will you go to Him, because you *must* or you will *die*? Will you go to Him? He did die for your struggles. He did and He *will* rescue you if you will go.

About the Author

Jamie's passion for life, Christ and others is evident in her smile, her transparency, and her ability to relate to others. When she asked the Lord, many years ago, why she had so much to say, He replied, "Because I want you to 'put them to rote.'" So came *Ahab and Jezebel* out of misery to ministry. Jamie promises there is more to come as the words and inspiration keep flooding in. Her heart's desire when writing and speaking to women is to usher them into the presence of their Savior.

Her leisure time is spent hiking, reading, and nurturing relationships.

Jamie lives in Arizona with her husband of thirty-seven years. They have three daughters, five sons-in-love, and nine grandchildren.

Contact the Author

Email:
jcistalkinboutit@yahoo.com

Website:
jamieclagueministries.com